Amy Friend

intentional
PIECING

Published in 2016 by Lucky Spool Media, LLC
www.luckyspool.com
info@luckyspool.com

Text © Amy Friend

Editor: Susanne Woods

Design: Page + Pixel

Illustrations: Kari Vojtechovsky

Photographer: Amy Friend

9 8 7 6 5 4 3 2 1
First Edition
Printed in the USA

Library of Congress Cataloging-in-Publication Data available upon request

ISBN 978-1-940655-18-5

LSID0030

Table of Contents

introduction

One of my vivid childhood memories is following my mother through the house as she was doing chores saying "I want to make something but I don't know what." My poor mother. I probably remember that so clearly because it happened for years on end. As a mother of three myself, I now feel badly that I pestered my mother like that, but I recall feeling very unsettled. Even back then, I wanted to create something, and I needed a plan.

I was a very good student, and my favorite assignments were things like dioramas, 3-D projects, posters, and any kind of creative competition. My love of both academics and art created a tug-of-war inside me. I felt the desire to use my academic ability in a meaningful way and also felt that ever-present nagging to create. When I enrolled in college, I took a class in Islamic art history my first semester as a freshman. I was hooked! Art history allowed me to harness my creativity through researching art objects. I pursued my master's coursework in American art history and material culture and went on to work as a collections curator in museums. I felt that I had achieved the balance I was looking for. I loved the academic rigor of research, documentation and writing. I loved the creativity involved in staging an exhibit, and the hands-on construction of storage mounts.

Becoming a mother changed things for me. I had always known that I wanted to be home raising my children when that time came. But I did miss the academics and the creativity I had enjoyed in my profession. I dabbled for a time in printmaking when my eldest was a baby. Once he began walking, I realized that wet ink was just asking for trouble. I needed something I could pick up and put down.

I had learned to sew as a child. When I was about four years old, my mom helped me hand stitch a little felt Pooh Bear. She also taught me the basics of garment sewing over the years. I made simple garments, appliqués, pillows, and later curtains for my home. Without analyzing it, I just decided to sew more. I discovered the modern quilting movement online and I was hooked once again.

At this point, I can say that fabric is my artistic medium of choice. When sewing, I approach my design and fabric selections just as I would for any artistic project. Because I have worked creatively all my life, be it in an art studio or in

What would make this design better? What design would really showcase this fabric?

my sewing room, my process feels intuitive. Though when I think about it, it's clear that I am constantly asking myself certain questions and basing my choices and decisions on my answers. I ask myself, What fabric would make this design better? What design would really showcase this fabric? What choices would make this project uniquely mine? I am exploring those questions in this book and hope to help my readers answer those questions for themselves as they join fabrics and patterns together to create projects that suit their personality and artistic visions. The designs in this book focus on this marriage of fabric and design. It's about fussy cutting, working with directional prints, stripes, textured solids and gradients, and even the use of selvages.

These days I rarely find myself thinking "I want to make something, but I don't know what." Now it's a question of how to find the time to sew up all the ideas! I am happy to share with you some of my ideas in this book and hope to inspire you to create.

Should you need any additional instructions along the way, please check out the free Quilt Making Basics PDF download available on the Lucky Spool site, www.luckyspool.com

what is intentional piecing anyway?

Intentional piecing is a conscious, deliberate process of fabric selection to suit a particular pattern design (or vice versa) or aesthetic. It is not scrappy or random but each choice is considered in order to find the best use for a special piece of fabric or fabrics that will highlight a pattern design. The work is planned with a specific outcome in mind. Every effort is made while piecing to place fabrics carefully and align them well within pattern boundaries for the intended effect.

TOOLS & EQUIPMENT

Like most of us, I'd rather be buying my favorite fabrics than stocking up on a lot of unnecessary tools and equipment, but there are a few basics that I use all the time. In addition to the standard quilt making tools that many of us already have, consider adding these piecing tools to your list of sewing room essentials. They each aid in ensuring accurate piecing and they won't break the bank.

foundation paper

There are many foundation papers on the market including transparent vellum, newsprint, and tear away type products. I find copy paper to be the least expensive option and I use it for all my paper piecing. It is less transparent but I like it for the stability it provides and the ease of paper removal. Like any of the materials I recommend, try a few products yourself and decide which you like best.

template plastic

Quilters' templates can be purchased alongside the marking pens, hand quilting hoops, and basting supplies in craft or quilt stores. They are made of a sturdy transparent plastic that is easily cut to size. When you are fussy cutting isolated images, it is helpful to place your template on the fabric to isolate motifs so you can center them precisely and know that they will fit within the seam allowance. It is also possible to use plastic packaging to do this.

tailor's chalk

When using a template, I like to mark the outer edge with chalk and use this as my cutting line. It is easily dusted off, but creates a visible line to follow. Hera markers are also a great alternative. These tools leave nice crease marks (no ink) that are easy to iron out.

embroidery
scissors

sewing
sheers

tailor's
chalk

needles

hera marker

rotary cutter

seam ripper

pins

quality iron

Pressing is so important. You need to love your iron. It doesn't matter what brand it is or how much you spend on it, as long as it gets nice and hot to press seams flat. An iron that has a little weight to it also seems to help.

starch

Sometimes steam can stretch piecing, and there is always the risk of your iron sputtering and making a mess of your piecing. I prefer to use a dry iron and starch. Starching helps reduce wrinkles that can cause inaccuracies in measurements and reduces the risk of stretching along bias seams. Also it keeps seams flat, which helps when nesting or matching seams. Grocery store starch is fine. It does the job and is inexpensive. You do have to be careful not to get flakes on your fabric while using it. Allowing the starch to dry before pressing will help. Other options are specialty products such as Mary Ellen's Best Press and Soak's Flatter.

cutting tools

There are a few critical cutting tools that should always be within reach.

EMBROIDERY SCISSORS

When I isolate fussy cuts with a plastic template as described above, I use a pair of sharp embroidery scissors because the fine tip is sharp enough to puncture the fabric along my chalk line, which allows me to cut around the motif without cutting from the edges of the fabric.

SEWING SHEERS

The brand isn't as important as how comfortable the sheers feel in your hand. You need to be able to work them easily and cut a smooth, accurate line when cutting around a motif for appliqué, for instance.

ROTARY CUTTER

The trusty rotary cutter is good for precutting fabric for piecing, trimming down to the ¼″ seam allowance as indicated on the foundation pattern, etc. Cutting through foundation paper will dull the blade quickly, but you can purchase a blade sharpener tool at your local quilt shop that works well to extend the life of each blade.

seam ripper

It is always worth taking the time to grab a seam ripper and restitch your piecing if your seams don't match or your directional print becomes skewed during sewing. I have never regretted taking the time to fix an imperfection. There are a variety of seam rippers on the market, from the economical to the truly artisan. Find one that feels comfortable and keep it handy during your piecing.

pins

I use two types of pin for quilting. The Clover flower head pins are long and sharp enough to work with multiple layers of fabric and foundation papers. I also like Clover fork pins, which are wonderful for matching up nesting seams and holding them securely in place while stitching.

needles

When paper piecing, I like to use Superior Thread's #90/14 topstitch titanium-coated needles. The large size of the needle makes bigger punctures in the foundation papers, making it easier to remove all that paper when you are done sewing. The titanium needles have a longer life span, which is particularly important here since sewing through paper dulls needles quickly.

hera marker

This sliglty odd looking tool can be useful for marking your fabrics without using a washable or disappearing marker. They create a crease on the surface of the fabric that is easily seen for cutting, but can be just as easily removed by ironing.

keeping organized

Because this book isn't about a race to the finish but rather intentional, thoughtful work, I suggest enjoying the process of selecting fabrics and stitching one block at a time. This also helps to keep things organized since the majority of the projects involve lots of small pieces and strategically selected fabric placement. Sometimes it is helpful to cut all the background pieces that are repeated from block to block; I just stack those with a Post-it note indicating the corresponding section number. Otherwise, I cut and piece a block at a time and enjoy the process of choosing the perfect fabrics to complete each block. I advise folding the scraps from each block and storing them in a 12" square scrapbooking plastic box until the project is complete — you may want to use certain fabrics again in later blocks so this prevents having to hunt for them in your stash.

paper piecing essentials

THE TECHNIQUE

1. To make a template, draw a 6½″ square on a piece of 20 lb. paper. Center a 6″ square inside that. From the lower left corner of the inner square, draw 4 lines using Figure 1 as a reference. Number each section (Fig. 1), making sure that you have at least ¼″ of fabric extending past the drawn lines.

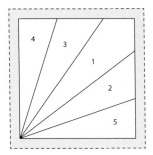

Figure 1

2. Cut your fabric a little bigger than you normally would for machine piecing. Beginning with Section 1, pin your fabric to

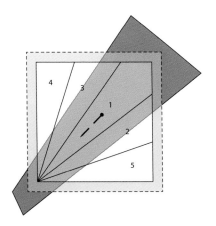

Figure 2

the wrong side of the template, leaving at least ¼″ of fabric extending past the drawn lines. The right side of the fabric should be facing up. (Fig. 2)

3. After ensuring that your fabric selection for Section 2 also has at least ¼″ around all sides (hold the layers up to a sunny window to check), place the fabric for Section 2 on top of the fabric for Section 1, right sides together. Pin in place if needed. Flip over your template so that the numbers are facing you and the fabric is on the bottom.

4. Set your machine's stitch length to 1.8 mm. This will make removing the template paper a lot easier. Sew along the line between Sections 1 and 2, extending into the seam allowance.

5. Fold the paper along the sewn line so that the right sides of the paper are facing. Use a ruler to measure ¼″ away from the sewn line onto the exposed fabric. Trim off the excess fabric with a rotary cutter and press open.

6. Repeat for all sections of the template, working in numerical order. (Fig. 3)

7. Press all seams again, this time on the right side of the fabric. (Fig. 4)

8. With the paper side facing up, trim around the template. Make sure to include any marked seam allowances. (Fig. 5)

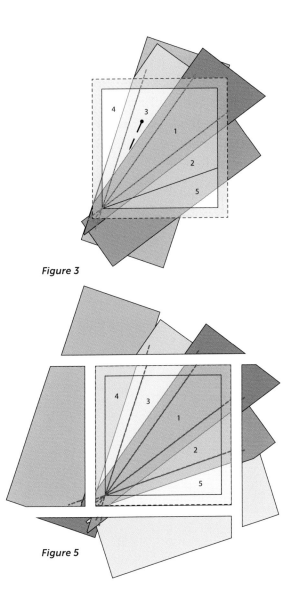

Figure 3

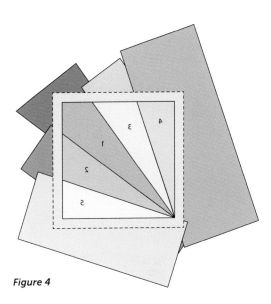

Figure 4

Figure 5

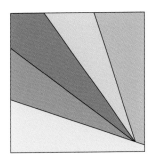

Finished Block

As you work to advance your paper piecing skills, there are some more things to think about. For this discussion, we will use B and C sections from the tee pee block from the My Tribe quilt (see page 42 and at right).

how to determine the dimensions of your fabric

Sometimes it can become unnecessarily intimidating to list cutting instructions for paper-pieced patterns with multiple pieces, and when there are many small pieces it just isn't feasible at all. If you need to determine the size of the fabric needed to cover a section, follow these simple instructions.

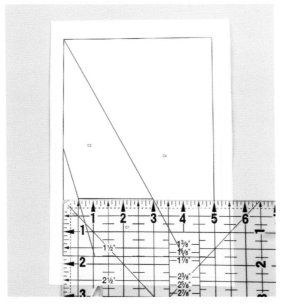

Figure 1

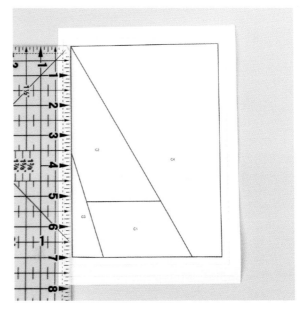

Figure 2

1. To determine the fabric needed to cover C2, first measure the width at the widest point and add ½" to each side (or a ¼" beyond the seam allowance). Here the widest point is 3" (Fig. 1). Adding ½" to each side gives you a 4" total fabric width.

2. Measure the height of the area at the tallest point and add a ½" to each side. Here the tallest point is about 5", so adding ½" to each side gives you 6". Thus, the fabric piece for C2 should be 4" × 6" (Fig. 2). Add a little more wiggle room to pieces that are angular and less for those that are straightforward piecing. I usually cut only enough pieces to stitch one block before cutting all the fabric for your quilt. You might find that you need a little more or less fabric for certain sections.

the importance of pressing

Pressing is critical when it comes to paper piecing. I often notice people not wanting to stop and press after each seam. However, let's look at Section B in the tee pee pattern template illustration (see right). These photographs illustrate what can happen if you quickly press or simply flip your fabric over.

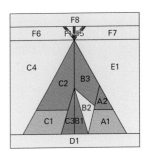

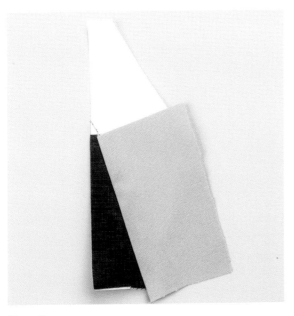

Figure 3

Figure 4

1. The tip of the tee pee door in Section B will need to meet the tip of the door in Section C.

2. Figure 3 looks okay until you tug at the fabric a little bit to reveal an extra ⅛'' of fabric hidden in the fold (Fig. 4). If left as is, the points couldn't possibly match. It's important to pull the fabric taut and press to maintain the integrity of the pattern. When matching points and something doesn't align, the first thing I look for is a pressing mistake.

Some sewists swear by their wooden seam rollers to press their seams, but I simply use my iron. I figure a little standing up and walking to the ironing board is good in a hobby where you are sitting for a long period of time! You might also consider setting up a pressing station near your sewing machine instead.

strike a pose!

It can be tricky to position your fabric to properly cover an angled section and/or to successfully line up a directional print.

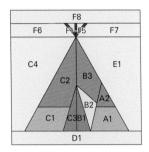

For this section, use the illustration of the tee pee block (above) as a reference, while we walk through how to position fabric to cover angled sections on a paper piecing template.

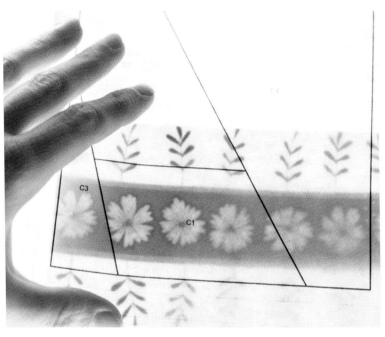

Figure 1

Refer to Section C1 in Figure 1. C1 is the fussy cut band at the bottom of the tee pee. Here, you can accurately position the fussy cut by using a light source.

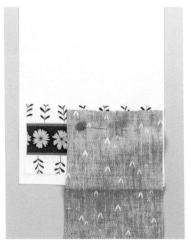

Figure 2

Figure 3

If you use a directional print or otherwise for the top of the tee pee, you simply line up your fabric to extend ¼'' over the seam line and the pin in place (Fig. 2). Sew, press and pin into place at the top of the section to reduce shift. (Fig. 3)

Figure 4

Section B isn't quite as simple, though. In order to keep the fabric directional for B3, insert a pin at the beginning and end of the line between B2 and B3, pin heads facing away from B3. (Fig. 4)

Figure 5

So that the fabric remains directional, adjust the fold to match the seam line, as indicated by the pins. (Fig. 5)

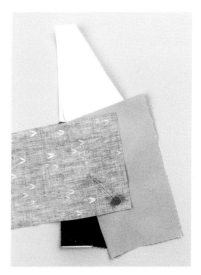

Figure 6

Carefully reach under the fold and hold the fabric with one hand while positioning the fabric with the other so that the right sides are facing. Pin into place and you are ready to stitch. (Fig. 6)

This will maintain the directionality. (Fig. 7)

Figure 7

A Finished Block

I leave my foundation papers in until my entire quilt top is sewn together. This prevents any stretching along the bias seams.

I do this every time I need to piece angular sections and/or to keep fabric on grain or directional. I hope you will find that this works for you too!

what to stash

BACKGROUNDS

My first love is paper piecing. I am always looking for a fabric that can handle being chopped up and seamed back together and appear cohesive, not chaotic, for the backgrounds of my blocks. I reach for textured solids, which add interest and dimension without the need to worry about directionality. Tone-on-tone prints such as a light text or newsprint, especially gravitating to those that are not directional or lined up in perfectly straight lines. Sometimes a small-scale print can serve this purpose too.

Another option is a print in which the designs are scattered enough so that I can use only the solid background for my tinier paper-pieced sections and control how the print is distributed in the rest. These textured solids, tonal prints and small-scale prints, are my sedums and daylilies (see Building Your Stash, page 19). They might not be the prints that strike me as the most exciting, but they make a significant contribution to the final outcome of the project. These fabrics I stash in at least half-yard pieces.

BLENDERS

I am always on the lookout for a good blending fabric or 'blender'. To keep my garden analogy going, (see Building Your Stash, page 19) I will compare them to hostas and other foliage plants in the garden. They are attractive in their own right but their main benefit is that they play well with others and help the flowering plants shine by providing a little space between colors in the garden or a difference in scale or foliage type. The majority of my stash is composed of blenders. I tend to buy them in half-yard pieces.

LARGE SCALE PRINTS

I tend to shy away from stashing large-scale prints. I think of them as showy annuals. When I need one as a focus print or for a quilt backing, I don't want to settle for something that is just 'close enough'. I like to purchase the perfect fabric at that time and in the quantity needed.

FUSSY CUTTING

Just as I seek the newest varieties of plants, I also seek quirky prints that are suitable for fussy cutting. I am drawn to text prints in all scales, as well as prints featuring labels. Sometimes I will pick up a print with an animal or house or other image that could easily be isolated and fussy cut. Having no plan for these prints and knowing that they often sit for quite a while before I find just the right project for them, I normally stash a fat quarter. Also, they tend to be the kind of prints that I need to include only in small doses for maximum impact. I might fussy cut a single word to really bring a design up a notch. Likewise, that uniquely colored coneflower can become a focal point of the garden, even if I only buy one.

It is so helpful and satisfying to have a well-rounded, usable stash to draw from while sewing. The Resources section (see page 114) includes the names of fabric shops that carry lots of quirky prints and textured solids. Happy shopping!

building your stash

I am often asked what I stash, how much, and why. You can come to the decision that is right for you if you follow my logic as I explain how I curate my own fabric collection. I love to garden, and I want all the flowers. But not all the flowers are useful to me given my soil conditions, moisture levels, sunlight, and zone. Sometimes I have to leave flowers behind at the nursery because I know I will not be able to put them to use in my yard. Again and again, I find myself purchasing another sedum or daylily in a new color or variety because those are my garden "go to's." They thrive in my dry, sunny, zone 5b garden.

Similarly, I want to buy every piece of fabric I love. However, I need to make choices. I have limited budget and space, and need to buy only those fabrics that I will actually use.

THE
projects

Magnetic Pin Tray

FINISHED SIZE: 5½" x 5½" x 1"

Most quilters love sewing-themed prints. The fabric companies seem hip to that and keep producing them. Quilters also love to make little gifts for their quilting friends. This project combines those two characteristics nicely. This Magnetic Pin Tray is easy to assemble, customizable, and the perfect project for sewing prints — and the rare earth magnets are cheaper when you buy them in quantity. It's a "win" all around.

This project is a comfortable way to ease into fussy cutting. You can narrow your fabrics to sewing-themed prints only, if fabric selection tends to overwhelm you and slow down the process of getting started. You need to find only two designs to isolate. By holding your template up to your fabric, you will be able to quickly identify the fabrics that will work well for this project. Once you choose your fussy cuts, use the color cues from those prints to choose the remaining fabrics.

MATERIALS
- **Template plastic**
- **Focus fabric:** fussy cut center, fussy cut corner squares
- **Inner Border fabric**
- **Outer Border fabric**
- **Backing fabric**

- **Tailor's chalk**
- **HeatnBond non-woven craft fusible interfacing**
- **Coordinating embroidery floss**

- **Hand-sewing needle**
- **1" x 2" x ¹⁄₁₆" grade N45 neodymium block rare earth magnet (see Resources, page 114)**

CUTTING

From template plastic, cut:
   (1) 2½" square
   (1) 1½" square

From focus fabric, cut:
   (1) 2½" fussy cut square using the template

   (4) 1½" fussy cut squares using the template

From inner border fabric, cut:
   (4) 2½" x 1½" rectangles

From outer border, cut:
   (2) 4½" x 1½" rectangles
   (2) 1½" x 6½" rectangles

From backing fabric, cut:
   (1) 6½" square

From fusible interfacing, cut:
   (1) 6" square

ASSEMBLING THE TRAY

Seam allowances are ¼" unless otherwise stated.

1. Referencing Figures 1 and 2 below, assemble the front panel, following the A-E piecing order and pressing the seams of your 9-Patch rows in opposite directions.

2. Following the manufacturer's instructions, center and fuse the interfacing to the wrong side of the backing fabric square leaving a ¼" around the fusible.

3. With right sides together, sew the tray block to the backing, (leaving a 3" opening on one side for turning). Clip the corners. (Fig. 3)

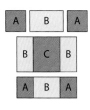

Figure 1

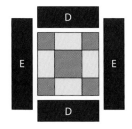

Figure 2

4. Turn right side out and press well pushing out the corners. Slip magnet into the opening. Pin around the magnet at the center of the pin tray so that it isn't accidentally drawn to the sewing needle as you stitch. (Fig. 4)

5. Edgestitch around the perimeter, and stitch in the ditch on just inside the outer border.

6. Pinch the corners of the tray block up, right sides together, at the width of the border strips. Stop at the outer corner of the squares. Using embroidery floss and a hand-sewing needle, stitch through the upper edge and secure with a square knot.

Figure 3

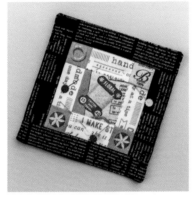

Figure 4

Hand stitching little Xs at the corners of the center square will help keep the magnet from sliding around and looks cute as well.

In the spirit of storytelling,
this quilt was photographed
with an alpaca. The alpaca
was very curious about the quilt
and I imagine her saying, "I see you are
quilter. I know a lot about yarn myself."

Tell Me a Story
Quilt

FINISHED BLOCK SIZE: 6″ SQUARE   **FINISHED QUILT SIZE:** 54″ x 60″

NUMBER OF BLOCKS: 56

One way to use fabric to its best advantage is to fussy cut motifs. Novelty fabrics often have small- to medium-size repeated motifs that can be easily isolated. I tend to lean toward quirky prints — especially those found in Japanese fabrics. I designed this quilt to feature a series of 3″ finished fussy cut designs, with each block telling its own story. (Fair warning: these blocks are addictive to make!)

Tell Me a Story is a process quilt. I hope you enjoy every minute of making it: taking your time combing through your stash, borrowing from your friends' stashes, turning your sewing room upside down looking for a particular print you know you have somewhere.

While the center squares and border prints coordinate to tell individual stories, the inner triangles and outer triangles are consistent to tie the scrappy blocks together. When it is time to arrange the blocks, simply spread out like colors and make sure that neighboring blocks don't clash. The wide borders unite the individual blocks, yet give them room to breathe.

MATERIALS

- **Template plastic**
- **Fussy cut prints**
- **Assorted prints for block borders**
- **Black fabric for innermost triangles:** ½ yard

- **Background fabric:** 2¼ yards
- **Backing fabric:** 3¾ yards cut in half and then seamed
- **Binding fabric:** ½ yard

- **Batting:** 60″ x 66″
- **Permanent marker**
- **Tailor's chalk**
- **20-lb. copy paper**

NOTE:

Use these templates to isolate fussy cuts. Using a permanent marker, draw the ¼″ seam allowance on your template. This allows you to accurately isolate your fussy cut area inside the drawn lines and be sure exactly what portion of the fabric will be visible when the block is sewn. Then, using tailor's chalk, trace around the template edge and cut on the drawn line. The template measurements listed include the seam allowance.

CUTTING

WOF = width of fabric

From template plastic, cut:
(1) 3½″ square

From fussy cut prints, use 3 ½″ plastic template square to cut:
(56) 3½″ center squares

From black fabric, cut:
(112) 2″ squares
  subcut each square on the diagonal

From assorted prints, cut:
(112) 2½″ x 3½″ strips
(112) 2½″ x 7½″ strips

From background fabric, cut:
(112) 3½″ squares
  subcut each square on the diagonal
(5) 6½″ x WOF strips for borders

intentional piecing

For this quilt, rather than following a prescribed color palette, I chose the fussy cuts from my stash randomly. When I work like this, I make each block work aesthetically on its own without giving a lot of thought to how it will look combined with other blocks. I enjoy making up little stories as I mull over my fabric selections. I might fussy cut a teacup for the center of my block and choose a text print with tea names as the border. That association is automatic and obvious. Other times, my stories are silly and a bit obscure. I chose a penguin with some text written on its belly for the center square, so for the border fabric, I used a light blue sky with white circles filled with text. I figured that a texty penguin would make texty snowballs, right?

PREPARATION

Make 56 copies of the foundation pattern (see page 116).

ASSEMBLING THE BLOCKS

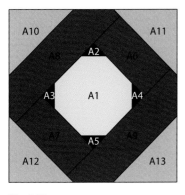

Block Diagram

Finished Block

For this project, I wouldn't recommend precutting all the blocks. Working one block at a time, from fabric selection straight through to the finished block, makes for a more enjoyable process.

1. Holding a paper template up to the light, position a center square within Section A1, on the side of the foundation without the printing. Secure with a pin.

2. Place the black triangles, aligning raw edges (A2, A3, A4, A5) with those of the center square and centering along that edge. Sew and press away from center square. (Fig. 1)

3. Pin a 2½'' x 3½'' block border strip overlapping ¼'' over the line for Sections A6 and A7, with right sides together. Sew and press away from the center square. (Fig. 2)

Figure 1

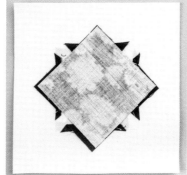

Figure 2

For foundation piecing, reduce your stitch length to about 1.8mm and use a size 90 needle for ease of paper removal.

4. Pin the 2½″ x 7½″ block border strip ¼″ over the seam line for Sections A9 and A8, with right sides together. Sew and press. (Fig. 3)

5. Pin the large background triangles with ¼″ extending over the seam lines, with right sides together. Sew and press. (Fig. 4)

6. Trim the block to include the ¼″ seam allowance.

7. Repeat to create a total of 56 blocks.

Figure 3

Figure 4

ASSEMBLING THE QUILT TOP

1. Referring to Figure 5, arrange the blocks in a 7 by 8 setting. Beginning at the upper left corner, stitch the blocks together to form the first row. Press the seams to the right in this row and all subsequent odd numbered rows. Press the seams of the even number rows to the left.

2. Sew the rows together. Press.

3. Assemble two border strips that measure 6½″ x 48½″. Sew them to the left and right sides. Press the seams toward the borders.

4. Assemble two strips that measure 6½″ x 54½″. Sew them to the top and bottom. Press the seams toward the borders.

FINISHING

1. Layer with batting and backing fabric, baste, and quilt as desired.

2. Attach binding using your favorite method.

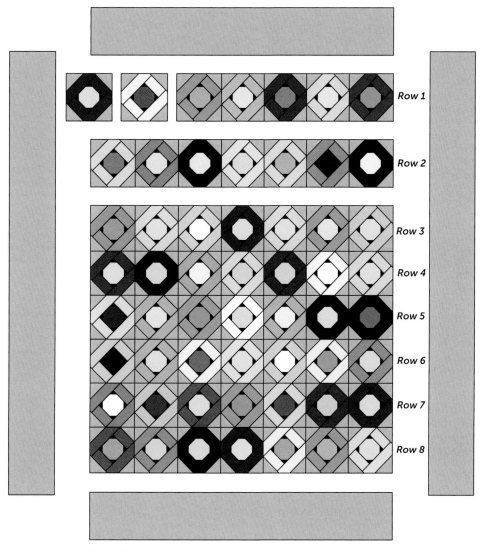

Row 1
Row 2
Row 3
Row 4
Row 5
Row 6
Row 7
Row 8

Figure 5

Adelaide Bag

FINISHED SIZE: 8½″ x 5″ x 1½″

This versatile zip bag is designed to showcase a fussy cut strip. So many fabrics have prints that can be isolated in this way. Once you start looking, you will realize how easy they are to find! This project works best with a strip design that is about 2½″ wide — this seems to be a common scale in fabric designs.

MATERIALS

- **Exterior fabric:** fat quarter
- **Lining fabric:** fat quarter
- **Focal fabric:** fussy cut 3″ x 5¼″ scrap
- **10″ zipper**
- **HeatnBond high-loft fusible fleece**

intentional piecing

I am sharing two versions of this project. One bag has gathers in the front and the other is flat fronted. The fussy cut is handled differently too, even though the same fabric is used. On the gathered version, the strip is cut in the more obvious way, to center a column of circles. On the flat-fronted bag, the strip is cut so that the negative space between two columns of circles is highlighted. In this case, the bag fabric is chosen to match that diamond shape created by the negative space to further define it as the focal point of the bag. The partial circles form a sort of scallop edge. The possibilities are unlimited!

CUTTING

Both Version A (flat) and Version B (gathered)

From focal fabric, cut:
    (1) 3" x 5¼" fussy cut strip

From exterior fabric, cut:
    1 piece using Template 1 (see page 119)

    (1) 4" x 2½" zipper cover

From lining fabric, cut:
    2 pieces using Template 1

From fusible fleece, cut:
    2 pieces using Template 1

Version A (flat)

From exterior fabric, cut:
    2 pieces using Template 2 (see page 117)

Version B (gathered)

From exterior fabric, cut:
    (2) 6" x 7" rectangles

PIECING THE BAG FRONT

Seam allowances are ¼" unless otherwise stated.

version A (flat)

1. Sew the two halves of the exterior front fabric onto the center strip, right sides together. Press away from the center strip.

2. Fuse to the fusible fleece.

3. Topstitch along the outer edges of the center strip. (Fig. 1)

Figure 1

version B (gathered)

1. To gather, set your machine to its longest stitch length, generally 5mm-6mm. On the 7″ side of the bag exterior rectangles, make two rows of gathering stitches, one at ¼″ and one at ⅜″ (Fig. 2). Adjust the gathers to fit the 5¼″ side of the fussy cut center strip and pin, right sides together. Stitch with a ½″ seam allowance. Repeat for the other side of the center strip. Press away from the center strip.

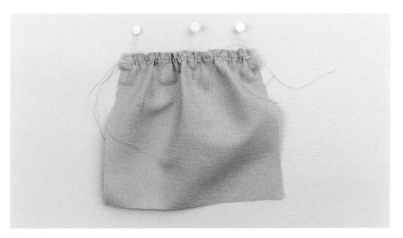

Figure 2

2. Find the center of one piece of fusible fleece. Mark the center of the fussy cut strip. Pin the fusible fleece, at top and bottom, to the bag front, matching centers. Adjust the gathers and press so that they fuse in place. Trim excess gathered fabric at the lower corners to match the curve of the fusible fleece.

3. Topstitch along the inner edges of the center strip.

ASSEMBLING THE BAG

both versions

1. Fuse the exterior back fabric to the fusible fleece.

2. Fold the zipper covers in half, wrong sides together, along the length. Then unfold and press long edges ¼" to the wrong side. Fold along center crease once more, raw edges enclosed. Cut zipper cover in half width-wise. Cut zipper just past the metal stop and cover that end with one zipper cover. Stitch close to the edge. Cut the zipper length as needed so that with the other zipper cover in place, the zipper unit measures 9". (Fig. 1)

3. Referencing the pattern piece (see page 117), mark the darts on the wrong side of the bag exterior and lining pieces. Match the lines with right sides together and stitch. (Fig. 2)

4. Position the bag front with the right side up. Place zipper unit with right side down and the pull on the left. Position lining with right side down (Fig. 3). Stitch ¼" along bag's upper edge through all layers. Press the lining under and topstitch along the zipper edge.

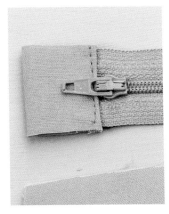

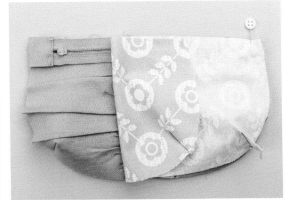

Figure 1   *Figure 2*   *Figure 3*

5. Repeat for the back side. Place the lining right side up, the zipper/bag unit right side up followed by the bag back, right side down (Fig. 4). Stitch ¼'' along bag's upper edge through all layers. Press lining under and topstitch along the zipper edge (Fig. 5).

6. Open the zipper at least halfway. Arrange both front and back units so that the bag exterior pieces are right sides together and lining pieces are also right sides together. Stitch around the perimeter, leaving an opening of about 3'' at the bottom of the linings for turning, backstitching at both ends of the seam. (Fig. 6)

7. Turn right side out, hand stitch the opening closed and push the lining inside the exterior.

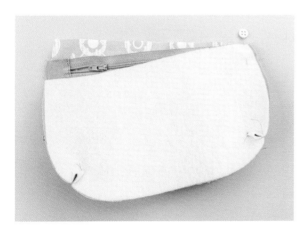

Figure 4

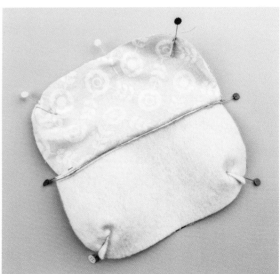

Figure 6

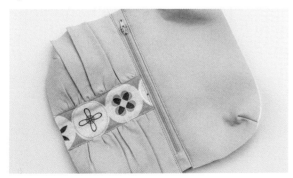

Figure 5

Appliqué Cardigan

I don't use a lot of appliqués in my quilting, but I do love to embellish my children's clothing with them. I have appliquéd pirates, dinosaurs, butterflies, sea horses, and more. This appliqué cardigan is an afternoon project that your child will love to wear over and over again!

MATERIALS

- **House fabric:** 7″ x 6″ scrap
- **Roof fabric:** 7″ x 3″ scrap
- **Window fabric:** 5″ x 2″ scrap
- **Chimney and door fabric:** 3″ square scrap
- **Various scraps for fussy cutting (optional)**
- **HeatnBond Lite fusible adhesive**
- **Cardigan coordinating thread**
- **Tiny button (optional)**

For this project, it's important to prewash your fabric and cardigan. This prevents uneven shrinking and allows the fusible to properly adhere.

intentional piecing

I chose to make a house, but there are endless possibilities. Just use your imagination! What about a firehouse with a fussy cut Dalmatian or a castle with a princess or even a barn with appliquéd animals? The cardigan used here is a size 7-8. You may need to adjust the size of your pattern pieces depending on the size cardigan you are using. Have fun selecting a variety of fabrics to create a scene of your own.

CUTTING

From house fabric, cut:
(2) 3'' x 5'' rectangles

From roof fabric, cut:
(2) 3¼'' x 2'' rectangles

From window fabric, cut:
(3) 1'' squares

From chimney and door fabric, cut:
(1) ¾'' x 1½'' rectangle for the chimney

(1) 1¼'' x 2¼'' rectangle for the door

Additional fussy cuts for embellishment (optional)

Fussy Cut Embellishments

PREPARING THE APPLIQUÉS

1. Prior to cutting, apply fusible adhesive to the back of all scraps following the manufacturer's instructions.

2. Cut around your chosen appliqués, leaving about ¼'' of fabric around the design.

3. If you are replicating my design, cut the flowering shrub free-form.

4. To create the diagonal line of the roof in my design, on one end of each roof piece, measure in ¼'' from the upper corner and draw a line to the lower corner. Cut on the drawn line.

EMBELLISHING THE CARDIGAN

1. Align the two front panels of the cardigan so that the buttons are next to the button holes. Position it neatly on the ironing board. Iron to remove any wrinkles or creases and leave the cardigan in place.

2. Place your appliqués on the cardigan to make sure you are happy with all your fabric choices, adjusting as necessary. (Fig. 1)

3. Peel the fusible backing off the appliqués. First fuse the house and roof pieces in place, making sure that the two sides meet up nicely across the center placket. Then fuse the smaller pieces, layering as necessary. (Fig. 2)

4. Machine stitch around each appliqué using coordinating thread colors and a narrow zigzag stitch. The setting used in this sample was a stitch with a width of 3.5mm and length of .70mm.

5. Final embellishments can be added using embroidery, additional decorative machine stitching, or even beads and buttons. I hand stitched a tiny button to the door for the door knob. (Fig. 3)

Figure 3

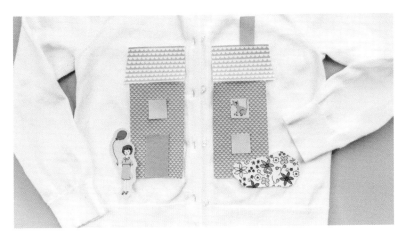

Figure 1

Figure 2

It is important to reduce the pressure of your presser foot while appliquéing so that the sweater doesn't get pulled out of shape. Another option is to use a fusible product on the back of the sweater to help keep the shape.

My Tribe Quilt

FINISHED BLOCK SIZE
TEE PEE BLOCKS: 10" SQUARE   **ARROW BLOCKS: 10" x 20"**

NUMBER OF BLOCKS
TEE PEE BLOCKS: 12   **ARROW BLOCKS: 2**

FINISHED QUILT SIZE: 40" x 40"

This baby-size quilt is appropriate for a nursery, but the design appeals to the young at heart as well. There are only two paper-pieced blocks in this quilt: the tee pee and the arrow. For consistency, the wooden poles at the top of each tee pee and the wood on the arrows are pieced using the same dark woodgrain print. Similarly, the door openings are all a black crosshatch. The tee pees are then pieced in various prints but limited within a color palette of turquoise, mint green, mustard, red, orange/red, silver, and peach.

MATERIALS

- **Background fabric:** 3 yards
- **Dark fabric for woodgrain:** ½ yard
- **Black crosshatch fabric for door openings:** ½ yard
- **Print fabrics for fussy cut borders:** a selection of 12, each measuring at least 10" x 2½"
- **Fabric for open tee pee doors:** a selection of 12 scraps, each measuring about 3" x 5"

- **Fabric for main tee pees:** a selection of 12 fat eighths
- **Fabric for arrow fletching:** a selection of 12 scraps, each measuring about 1¾" x 7"
- **Animal fabric to fussy cut**
- **Binding fabric:** ⅜ yard
- **Backing fabric:** 1¼ yards

NOTE If you plan to quilt this on a longarm, you will need to increase the backing yardage to 2½ yards.

- **Batting:** 46" x 46"
- **HeatnBond Lite fusible adhesive:** ¼ yard
- **20-lb. copy paper**

	TEE PEE BLOCKS	ARROW BLOCKS
From the background fabric, cut:	(24) 10½″ x 1½″ strips (D1, F8) (12) 8″ x 11″ rectangles	(10) 6¾″ x 5¼″ rectangles
	With 6 units right side up and 6 units wrong side up, subcut each rectangle on the diagonal 2⅛″ from upper-left corner and 2″ from lower-right corner (for E1 and C4) — or, if you prefer, simply work from an 11″ x WOF strip	With 5 units right side up and 5 units wrong side up, subcut each rectangle on the diagonal, placing the ruler 1″ to the right of the upper-left corner and the other end of the ruler 1″ up from the lower-right corner (A3, A4, A6, A7, A9, B3, B4, B6, B7, B9)
	(12) 2″ squares	(4) 5½″ x 10½″ rectangles (A1, B1) (2) 7½″ x 6½″ rectangles
	subcut each square on the diagonal (F2, F4)	subcut each rectangle on the diagonal (C1, C3)
From the dark woodgrain fabric, cut:	(36) ¾″ x 2″ strips (F1, F3, F5)	(2) 2″ x 17″ strips (A10)
From black crosshatch fabric, cut:	(24) 2½″ x 5″ rectangles (B1, C3)	(2) 11‴ x 5½″ rectangles (C2)
From fussy cut border print fabrics, cut:	(12) 10″ x 2½″ strips (A1, C1)	
From open tee pee door fabrics, cut:	(12) 3″ x 5″ rectangles (B2)	
From main tee pee fabrics, cut:	(12) 3″ squares (A2) (12) 3½″ x 6½″ rectangles (B3) (12) 4½″ x 6½″ rectangles (C2)	
From arrow fletching fabrics, cut:	(12) 1¾″ x 7″ strips (A2, A5, A8, B2, B5, B8)	

intentional piecing

This quilt provides a good opportunity to use a subtle directional fabric for the background and the tee pees each have a stripe along the base — the perfect opportunity for fussy cutting! I used a couple of prints with repeated rows of designs and fussy cut different portions of them for each tee pee, making it appear that several different fabrics had been used.

PREPARATION FOR THE TEE PEE BLOCKS

1. Make 12 copies of the tee pee foundation pattern and 2 copies of the arrow foundation pattern (see pages 118-121).

2. Before assembling the tee pee blocks, decide if you want to include fussy cut animals peeking from behind the tee pees. If so, decide how many and in what locations and find animals of the correct scale to fussy cut. See page 40 for applique instructions.

When selecting an appliqué, make sure that the color of the fabric background doesn't contrast too sharply with your block background. This will give the impression of a cutout.

Tips for Appliqué

- It is easiest to fussy cut animals peeking from the right side of the tee pee since Section E1 is its own piece. Fuse your animals to HeatnBond Lite, a fusible adhesive. Using sharp scissors, carefully cut around the edge of your appliqué, leaving about ⅛" to ¼" of background fabric around the animals. The less background fabric, the more the fussy cut will blend into the background, but it is also more difficult to sew. Try to round any sharp edges, so that following them with your sewing machine won't be too difficult. For example, do not cut deeply into a concave curve — instead, round the line to make stitching more successful.

- Position the animals on the fabric that will be used for either Section C4 or E1 (see block diagram on page 46). Hold them up to the paper pattern, making sure that you take note of the seam allowances so that nothing will get cut off when the block is sewn together. Fuse the appliqué with your iron.

- Stitch around the edges. I thought that a zigzag stitch would make the outline too harsh here, so I used a straight stitch instead to create a raw-edge appliqué. Sometimes I do this with my free-motion foot — here I used my regular straight stitch but shortened the stitch length to 2mm to make accuracy easier. This way I have accuracy but also an even stitch length. The start and stop of your stitching will be sewn into the seam allowance.

3. Refer to page 45 to see a prepared appliqué on Section E1 ready to be sewn to a completed Section A2. Note that a pin is used to hold the larger paper-pieced sections to the pattern. This helps to keep them from slipping away from the seam allowance when you sew the block together and aids in accuracy.

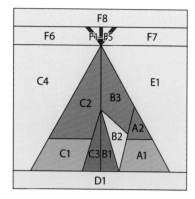

Block Diagram

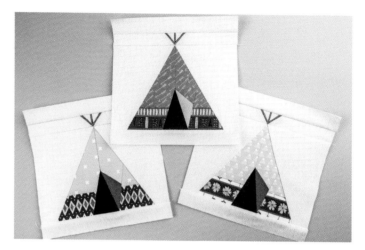

Finished Blocks

ASSEMBLING THE TEE PEE BLOCKS

1. Referring to the Block Diagram for fabric placement, paper piece each section of the tee pee block.

2. Position completed sections with right side down and, using your ruler, trim the block along the ¼'' seam allowance as indicated on the pattern.

3. Assemble the block by sewing Section A to B to E and then to C. Next sew on a 10½'' x 1½'' strip for Section D1. You do not need to use the paper pattern for this as the section is rotary cut to the exact dimensions.

4. Sew Section F to the completed lower portion of the block. Press.

5. Repeat to create a total of 12 tee pee blocks.

ASSEMBLING THE ARROW BLOCKS

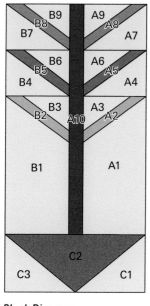

Block Diagram

Finished Block

1. Referring to the Block Diagram for fabric placement, paper piece each section of the arrow block.

2. Position completed sections with right side down and, using your ruler, trim the block along the ¼″ seam allowance as indicated on the pattern.

3. Assemble the block by sewing Section A to B and then to C. Press.

4. Repeat to make 2 arrow blocks.

ASSEMBLING THE QUILT TOP

1. Referring to Figure 1, sew the blocks together by first stiching the tee pee units into three vertical pairs, one horizontal pair and one strip of 4 blocks. Assemble into three rows, pressing the seams in alternate directions. Finally, stitch the rows together to form the quilt top.

FINISHING

1. Layer with batting and backing fabric, baste, and quilt as desired.

2. Attach the binding using your favorite method.

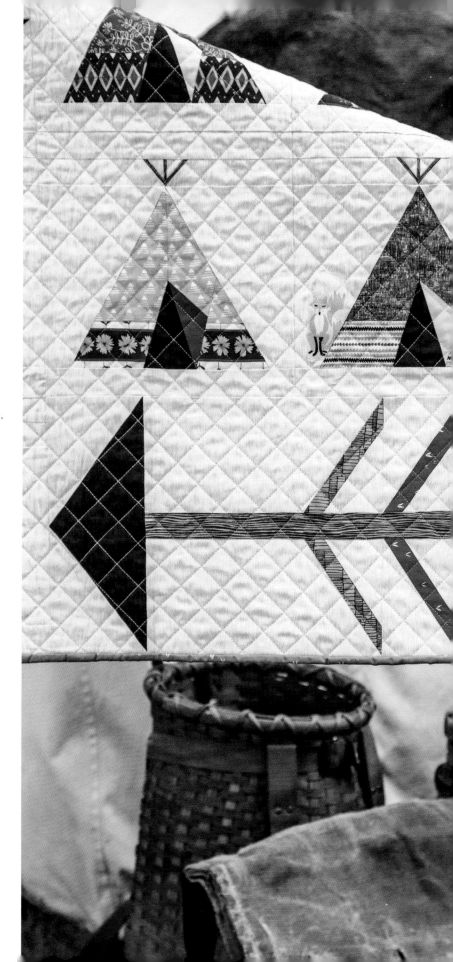

Figure 1

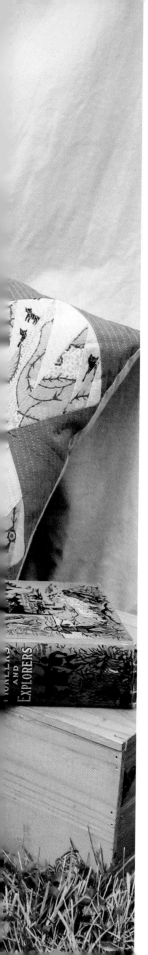

Grasslands Pillow

FINISHED PILLOW SIZE: 18″ SQUARE

We tend make our fabric choices after we look at the scale of a block design. You might have the perfect little scrap of fabric that just doesn't fit and you have to set it aside, disappointed. But what if you simply adjusted the pattern to suit your fussy cut instead? This can expand your options exponentially. In the case of this block, I was looking for grassland animals that I could position behind the blades of grass, as if they were peeking out at you. I found three animal prints of different scales that I wanted to use so I experimented with the block size until I found one that worked best for each print. When you take control over not only your fabric choices but the scale of the pattern, it's really liberating. Suddenly, so many more opportunities open up.

What's your favorite animal? Have fun hunting for a great fabric to fussy cut for your pillow. The motif you choose may fit well into one of the versions — if not, use these patterns as a base, and remember that the scale can determine the design.

MATERIALS

All Versions

- **Assorted scraps for blades of grass**
- **Assorted scraps of solids for spaces between grass as required**
- **Main fabric for fussy cutting**
- **Backing fabric:** ⅝ yard
- **Binding fabric:** ¼ yard (optional)
- **HeatnBond high-loft fusible fleece**
- **18″ square pillow form**

Version A (tiger pillow, using 4 blocks finishing at 8″ each)

- **Fabric for outer triangles:** ⅜ yard
- **Front sashing fabric:** ⅛ yard

Version B (lion pillow, using 1 block finishing at 11″)

- **Front sashing/outer triangle fabric:** ½ yard

Version C (zebra pillow, using 1 block finishing at 16″)

- **Fabric for front outer corners:** ⅜ yard

CUTTING

WOF = width of fabric

All Versions

From the backing fabric, cut:

(2) 18½″ x 13″ rectangles

From the binding fabric (optional), cut:

(2) 2½″ x WOF strips for binding

Version A (tiger pillow)

From outer triangle fabric, cut:

(8) 5″ squares

subcut each square on the diagonal

From front sashing fabric, cut:

(2) 1½″ x 16½″ strips

(2) 18½″ x 1½″ strips

Version B (lion pillow)

From outer triangle/front sashing fabric, cut:

(2) 6″ squares

subcut each square on the diagonal

(1) 2½″ x 11½″ strip

(1) 5½″ x 11½″ rectangle

(1) 18½″ x 3½″ rectangle

(1) 18½″ x 4½″ rectangle

Version C (zebra pillow)

From front outer corners fabric, cut:

(2) 12″ squares

subcut each square on the diagonal (take care when cutting on the diagonal if you are using a directional print)

PREPARATION

Make copies of the foundation pattern (see pages 122-124):

Version A (tiger pillow): 4 copies enlarged by 150%, 8″ finished block

Version B (lion pillow): 1 copy enlarged by 125% to make it an 11″ finished block

Version C (zebra pillow): 1 copy enlarged by 182% and taped together to make it a 16″ finished block

There are online tools available for calculating the proper enlargement percentage. You need to know the size of the block you are starting with, in this case 8″, and the size you wish to make. The program will calculate the exact enlargement percentage necessary. http://news.rapidresizer.com/2012/10/how-to-enlarge-a-pattern-by-percent-or-scale.html

intentional piecing

The yardage required for each pillow varies depending on the layout of the animals on the fabric. In the case of the lion pillow, the lions were scattered through the print along with a pattern of leaves and flowers. It was easy to piece one section using the lion head, but problematic to avoid the lions and just use the leaves/flowers for the other pieces. The tigers were spaced too closely so I used a matching pale pink solid for the spaces between the grass that were not going to include fussy cut tigers. For the zebra pillow I used mostly the zebra-printed fabric but I also put in a little bit of plain linen because it was impossible to fussy cut a section that did not include some part of the zebra. The zebra print was directional too—some zebras faced right and others left. Because my fussy cut zebra faced right, I needed to use two different zebras for the fussy cutting — one for the head and tail and another for the center of the body.

ASSEMBLING THE PILLOW FRONT

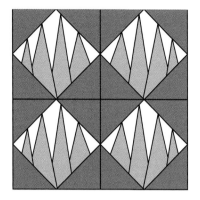

Block Diagram

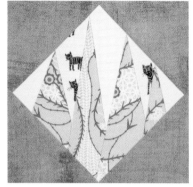

Finished Block

If you are new to paper piecing, it's important to know that smaller blocks are actually less difficult to sew because the fabric pieces are easier to manipulate.

version A (tiger pillow)

1. The tiger pillow is sewn from the 8″ block. I don't recommend making the block any smaller because there isn't a lot of room for fussy cut animals even at the 8″ size. The pillow is constructed using 4 blocks, 2 original orientations and 2 mirror images. I did this so that there is some variety in the position of grass blades from block to block. Tigers are fussy cut behind some of the blades of grass, and a coordinating solid was used behind others. In this instance, the same print was used for all the blades of grass and a textured solid for the outer triangles.

2. Paper piece each of the 4 blocks. Position each block fabric side down and trim down to the ¼″ seam allowance as indicated on the pattern.

3. Referencing the Block Diagram above, sew the blocks together into a 4-Patch, being sure to press seams in alternate directions for your columns and rows so that your seams nest nicely.

4. Sew the shorter side sashing strips to either side of the block and press the seams toward the sashing.

5. Sew the longer sashing strips to the top and bottom of the block and press the seams toward the sashing.

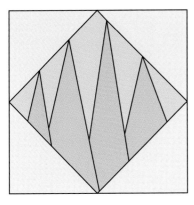

Block Diagram

Finished Block

version B (lion pillow)

1. Paper piece the 11″ block. Position the block, fabric side down, and trim ¼″ from the line marking the finished block. Because the block has been enlarged, the outer ¼″ seam marking is no longer accurate.

2. The block is positioned off center on the pillow front using borders. Sew the 2½″ x 11½″ rectangle to the left side of the block. Press the seam allowance away from the block.

3. Sew the 5½″ x 11½″ rectangle to the right side of the block. Press the seam allowance away from the block.

4. Sew the 18½″ x 3½″ strip to the top of the block. Press the seam allowance away from the block.

5. Sew the 18½″ x 4½″ strip to the bottom of the block. Press the seam allowance away from the block.

Finished Pillow Top

version C (zebra pillow)

1. Using the pattern enlarged to a 16″ block, paper piece the central on-point square only. This zebra print is such a large scale that the zebra is pieced across three sections. This requires extra yardage because you need to cut into a few zebras in order to create the body of just one.

2. Rather than adding the outer triangles and trimming down to the ¼″ seam allowance, sew the large corner triangles around the center block. They will extend beyond the block and overlap each other.

3. Position the block with the fabric side down and line up the 1¼″ line on your ruler with the finished block edge as indicated on the pattern. Trim. Repeat on all 4 sides.

all versions

All three versions can be finished following the same directions since they each measure 18½″ unfinished.

1. Fuse the finished block to an 18½″ square of fusible fleece following the manufacturer's directions. The fleece keeps all your seams fused in place and adds substance to the pillow front.

2. Quilt as desired. In Version A (tiger), I quilted the pillow with tightly spaced diagonal lines. The diagonal quilting is used again in Version B (lion) but only in the background fabric. The blades of grass are quilted with free-motion wavy lines. Sharp but varied blades of grass are quilted into the pieced grass of Version C, and diagonal lines are used in the outer triangles.

FINISHING AS AN ENVELOPE-BACK SLIPCOVER PILLOW

1. Make a double hem on one long side of a back panel rectangle by folding one 18½" edge in ¼" and pressing with an iron. Fold the edge another ¼" and press. Topstitch ⅛" away from folded edge. Repeat with the second back panel.

2. Lay your finished pillow front facing up.

3. With right sides together, align one back panel rectangle with the left edge of the pillow front, raw edges aligned. Align the other back panel with the right edge of the pillow front. The finished edges of the back panel rectangles will overlap. (Fig. 1)

4. Pin around all 4 sides and sew using a ¼" seam. Clip away the corner points, being careful not to cut into the seam.

5. Turn right side out and insert the pillow form.

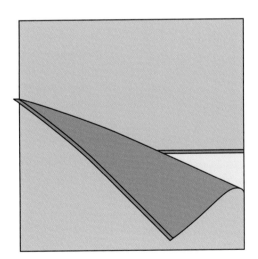

Figure 1

Alternately, should you want to bind the edges of the pillow cover, place the overlapped pillow back pieces wrong sides together with the pillow front. Baste around the edge. Then create a length of binding using (2) 2½" x WOF strips and stitch around the pillow front, hand finishing on the back, just as you do a quilt binding.

Transatlantic Quilt

FINISHED SIZE: 60″ x 70″ • **NUMBER OF BLOCKS: 36**

Looking at my stash, I realized that I had an extensive collection of map, postage, airmail and other travel-related prints. It was when I was thinking about how to use them all that Transatlantic was born. I decided on a rather busy map background so in contrast, I kept my suitcases bold and simple. The map print is directional but forgiving. Not all the lines on the print are perfectly horizontal/vertical, making it a great choice for a paper-pieced background. Wouldn't it be fun to make a quilt like this as a memento of your own travels, or maybe as a meaningful gift for someone who loves to travel?

MATERIALS

- **Background fabric:** 5 yards

- **White fabric for airmail envelope:** 1 yard

- **Prints for airmail envelope border:** 2 prints, ½ yard each

- **Black fabric for airplane:** ½ yard

- **Backing fabric:** 4¼ yards

- **Binding fabric:** ½ yard

- **Batting:** 66″ x 76″

Materials vary by block based on your choice of prints and how much fabric you have to "waste" to make your fussy cuts. We only list the yardage here for the fabrics that are used in more than one of the block designs.

PREPARATION

Make copies of the foundation patterns (see pages 125-138). The instructions for each block are separated below by block type. This allows you to create the quilt one block at a time, or focus on creating one particular block for use in a different project.

intentional piecing

You will need an assortment of travel-themed prints, specifically airmail arrows, stamps, addresses, etc. If you don't have a large stash to access, consider purchasing a fat quarter bundle in a travel and/or airmail theme that you love. There are often new fabric collections based on those themes. Also seek out Japanese prints because they often include text with names of geographical locations and stamps.

SUITCASE 1 BLOCK

FINISHED BLOCK SIZE: 10" SQUARE • **NUMBER OF BLOCKS: 3**

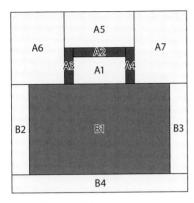

Block Diagram Suitcase 1

Finished Block

This suitcase is perfect for a large-scale travel print that you can't bear to chop up or a print that won't hold its own against the background if broken up.

assembling the suitcase 1 block

1. Referring to the Block Diagram Suitcase 1, paper piece each section of the block.

2. Position the completed section with right side down and, using your ruler, trim the block along the ¼" seam allowance as indicated on the pattern.

3. Assemble the block by sewing Section A to B. Press.

4. Repeat to create a total of 3 blocks.

CUTTING

From the background fabric, cut:

(3) 4" x 2½" rectangles (A1)

(3) 5" x 3" rectangles (A5)

(6) 4" x 5" rectangles (A6, A7)

(6) 2" x 6" strips (B2, B3)

(3) 11" x 2" strips (B4)

From the main fabric, cut:

(3) 9" x 6" rectangles (B1)

From the handle fabric, cut:

(9) 3½" x 1½" strips (A2, A3, A4)

SUITCASE 2 BLOCK

FINISHED BLOCK SIZE: **10" SQUARE**   •   **NUMBER OF BLOCKS:** **6**

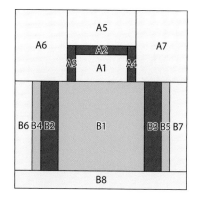

Block Diagram Suitcase 2

Finished Block

CUTTING

From the background fabric, cut:

(6) 4" x 2½" rectangles (A1)

(6) 5" x 3" rectangles (A5)

(12) 4" x 5" rectangles (A6, A7)

(12) 2" x 6" strips (B6, B7)

(6) 11" x 2" strips (B8)

From the main fabric, cut:

(6) 6" squares (B1)

(12) 1½" x 6" strips (B4, B5)

From the accent fabric, cut:

(12) 2" x 6" strips (B2, B3)

From the handle fabric, cut:

(18) 3½" x 1½" strips (A2, A3, A4)

These suitcases are the same as Suitcase 1 but they have accent straps. The accent straps allow for some fussy cutting. In one case, I used metallic Xs to look like metal brads and, in others, place names. Because the body of the suitcase is divided, a solid fabric choice helps hold the design together.

assembling the suitcase 2 block

1. Referring to the Block Diagram Suitcase 2 above, paper piece each section of the block.

2. Position the completed section with right side down and, using your ruler, trim the block along the ¼" seam allowance as indicated on the pattern.

3. Assemble the block by sewing Section A to B. Press.

4. Repeat to create a total of 6 blocks.

SUITCASE 3 BLOCK

FINISHED BLOCK SIZE: **10″ SQUARE**   •   **NUMBER OF BLOCKS:** **3**

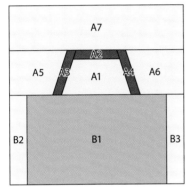

Block Diagram Suitcase 3

Finished Block

CUTTING

From the background fabric, cut:
   (3) 5″ x 3½″ rectangles (A1)

   (6) 4½″ x 3½″ rectangles (A5, A6)

   (3) 11″ x 3½″ strips (A7)

   (6) 2″ x 6″ strips (B2, B3)

From the main fabric, cut:
   (3) 9″ x 6″ rectangles (B1)

From the handle fabric, cut:
   (9) 3½″ x 1½″ strips (A2, A3, A4)

Like Suitcase 1, Suitcase 3 is perfect for a large-scale travel print or one that will not hold its own against the background if broken up. A print of similar value to the background fabric would work nicely here.

assembling the suitcase 3 block

1. Referring to the Block Diagram Suitcase 3 above, paper piece each section of the block, consulting the block diagram for fabric placement.

2. Position the completed section with right side down and, using your ruler, trim the block along the ¼″ seam allowance as indicated on the pattern.

3. Assemble the block by sewing Section A to B. Press.

4. Repeat to create 3 blocks.

SUITCASE 4 BLOCK

FINISHED BLOCK SIZE: 10″ SQUARE • **NUMBER OF BLOCKS: 4**

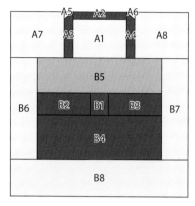

Block Diagram Suitcase 4

Finished Block

When choosing fabrics for this block, make sure the top and bottom fabrics of the suitcase have good contrast. A busier print on the bottom half combined with a solid top can work well to achieve that contrast. These blocks are helpful in bringing a couple of colors from other parts of the quilt top together in one block that unites the entire quilt top.

assembling the suitcase 4 block

1. Referring to the Block Diagram Suitcase 4 above, paper piece each section of the block, consulting the block diagram for fabric placement.

2. Position the completed section with right side down and, using your ruler, trim the block along the ¼″ seam allowance as indicated on the pattern.

3. Assemble the block by sewing Section A to B. Press.

4. Repeat to create a total of 4 blocks.

CUTTING

From the background fabric, cut:
- (4) 4″ x 3″ strips (A1)
- (8) 4″ x 3½″ rectangles (A7, A8)
- (4) 1½″ squares subcut each square on the diagonal (A5, A6)
- (8) 2½″ x 6½″ strips (B6, B7)
- (4) 11″ x 3″ strips (B8)

From the main fabrics, cut:
- (8) 4″ x 2¼″ strips (B2, B3)
- (4) 8″ x 3½″ rectangles (B4)

From the accent fabrics, cut:
- (4) 3″ x 8″ rectangles (B5)

From the buckle fabric, cut:
- (4) 2″ x 2½″ rectangles (B1)

From the handle fabric, cut:
- (12) 3½″ x 1½″ strips (A2, A3, A4)

AIRMAIL ENVELOPE AND FLAP BLOCK

FINISHED BLOCK SIZE: 10" SQUARE • **NUMBER OF BLOCKS: 3**

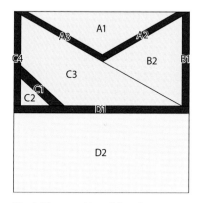

Block Diagram Airmail Envelope

Finished Block

CUTTING

From the background fabric, cut:
- (3) 11" x 5½" rectangles (D2)

From the white fabric, cut:
- (3) 9½" x 3½" rectangles (A1)
- (3) 5½" x 6" rectangles (B2)
- (2) 4" squares subcut each square on the diagonal (C2)
- (3) 11" x 6½" rectangles (C3)

From the border fabric, cut:
- (9) 1½" x 6½" strips (A2, B1, C4)
- (3) 1½" x 7½" strips (A3)
- (3) 1½" x 11" strips (D1)
- (3) 1½" x 4½" strips (C1)

It can be tricky to line up the airmail border print for these blocks, but accurate alignment is what makes this block look so great! Follow my suggestions on Paper Piecing Essentials (see page 16) to help achieve that accuracy here.

assembling the airmail envelope and flap block

1. Referring to the Block Diagram Airmail Envelope above, paper piece each section of the block, consulting the block diagram for fabric placement.

2. Position the completed section with right side down and, using your ruler, trim the block along the ¼" seam allowance as indicated on the pattern.

3. Assemble the block by sewing Section A to B to C to D. Press.

4. Repeat to create a total of 3 blocks.

AIRMAIL ENVELOPE AND STAMP BLOCK

FINISHED BLOCK SIZE: 10″ SQUARE • **NUMBER OF BLOCKS: 5**

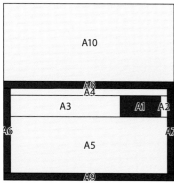

Block Diagram Airmail and Stamp

Finished Block

CUTTING

From the background fabric, cut:

   (5) 11″ x 5½″ rectangles (A10)

From the white fabric, cut:

   (5) 1½″ x 2″ strips (A2)

   (5) 7½″ x 2″ rectangles (A3)

   (5) 10″ x 1½″ strips (A4)

   (5) 10″ x 4″ rectangles (A5)

From the fussy cut stamp fabric, cut:

   (5) 3¼″ x 2¼″ rectangles (A1)

From the border print fabric, cut:

   (10) 1½″ x 5½″ strips (A6, A7)

   (10) 11″ x 1½″ strips (A8, A9)

There are lots of fabric designs with stamps, but the stamp you want to use might not fit perfectly within Section A1. You may need to adjust the lines surrounding Section A1 in order to make your favorite fabric work.

assembling the airmail envelope and stamp block

1. Referring to the Block Diagram Airmail and Stamp above, paper piece the block, consulting the block diagram for fabric placement.

2. Position the completed block with right side down and, using your ruler, trim the block along the ¼″ seam allowance as indicated on the pattern.

3. Repeat to create a total of 5 blocks.

LUGGAGE TAG BLOCK

FINISHED BLOCK SIZE: 10″ SQUARE • **NUMBER OF BLOCKS: 1**

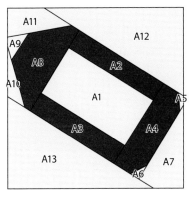

Block Diagram Luggage Tag

Finished Block

CUTTING

From the background fabric, cut:

(1) 2″ square subcut on the diagonal (A5, A6)

(1) 3½″ x 5½″ rectangle (A7)

(1) 2″ x 3″ rectangle (A9)

(1) 2″ x 4½″ rectangle (A10)

(1) 4½″ x 2½″ rectangle (A11)

(1) 10½″ square subcut on the diagonal (A12, A13)

From the main fabric, cut:

(2) 6½″ x 2″ strips (A2, A3)

(1) 2½″ x 6½″ strip (A4)

(1) 3½″ x 6½″ rectangle (A8)

From the address fabric, cut:

(1) 6½″ x 4″ rectangle (A1)

Choose a text fabric with an address for the fussy cut luggage tag. If you can't find just the right fabric, try stamping on fabric using fabric inks and heat setting the stamped words with your iron. Or embroider words. You could use this block as your quilt label and include your name, the title of the quilt, date made, etc.

assembling the luggage tag block

1. Referring to the Block Diagram Luggage Tag above, paper piece the block, consulting the block diagram for fabric placement.

2. Position the completed block with right side down and, using your ruler, trim the block along the ¼″ seam allowance as indicated on the pattern.

FLY BLOCK

FINISHED BLOCK SIZE: 20″ x 8″ • **NUMBER OF BLOCKS: 1**

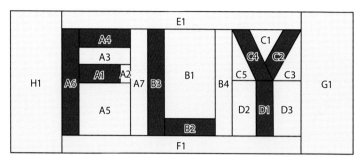

Block Diagram FLY

assembling the FLY block

1. Referring to the Block Diagram Fly above, paper piece each section of the block, consulting the block diagram for fabric placement.

2. Position the completed section with right side down and, using your ruler, trim the block along the ¼″ seam allowance as indicated on the pattern.

3. Assemble the block by sewing Section A to B. Set aside. Sew Section C to D. Sew AB to CD, then attach E and F, and finally attach G and H. Press.

CUTTING

From the background fabric, cut:

(1) 1½″ x 2″ rectangle (A2)

(1) 4″ x 2″ rectangle (A3)

(1) 4″ square (A5)

(2) 2″ x 7″ strips (A7, B4)

(1) 4″ x 6″ rectangle (B1)

(1) 3″ x 4″ rectangle (C1) subcut on the diagonal (C3, C5)

(2) 2½″ x 4″ rectangles (D2, D3)

(2) 21″ x 2″ strips (E1, F1)

(2) 4″ x 9″ rectangles (H1, G1)

From the letter fabric, cut:

(6) 4½″ x 2″ strips (A1, A4, B2, C2, C4, D1)

(2) 7″ x 2″ (A6, B3)

AIRPLANE BLOCK

FINISHED BLOCK SIZE: 20" x 12" • **NUMBER OF BLOCKS: 1**

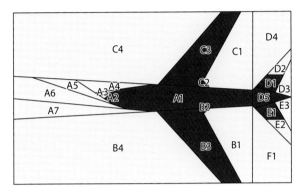

Block Diagram Airplane

assembling the airplane block

1. Referring to the Block Diagram Airplane above, paper piece each section of the block, consulting the block diagram for fabric placement.

2. Position the completed section with right side down and, using your ruler, trim the block along the ¼" seam allowance as indicated on the pattern.

3. Assemble the block by sewing Section A to B to C. Set aside. Sew Section D to E to F. Sew both sections together. Press.

CUTTING

From the background fabric, cut:

For all of the A sections cut from scraps, since they are so oddly shaped

(2) 4½" x 6½" rectangles (B1, C1)

(2) 16½" x 6½" rectangles (B4, C4)

(1) 3" square (D2, E2)

(2) 2½" x 3½" rectangles (D3, E3)

(1) 4" x 7" rectangle (D4, F1)

From the black fabric, cut:

(1) 10" x 3" rectangle (A1)

(2) 4" x 8" rectangles (B3, C3)

(2) 3" x 2" rectangles (D1, E1)

B2 and C2 sections from cut-offs

(1) 4" x 2½" rectangle (D5)

MOUNTAIN RANGE BLOCK

FINISHED BLOCK SIZE: 20" x 12" • **NUMBER OF BLOCKS: 1**

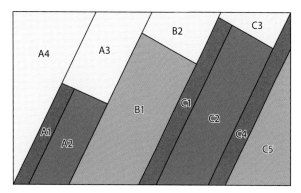

Block Diagram Mountain Range

assembling the mountain range block

1. Referring to the Block Diagram Mountain Range above, paper piece each section of the block, consulting the block diagram for fabric placement.

2. Position the completed section with right side down and, using your ruler, trim the block along the ¼" seam allowance as indicated on the pattern.

3. Assemble the block by sewing Section A to B to C. Press.

CUTTING

From the background fabric, cut:

(1) 8" x 14" rectangle (A4)

(1) 7" x 8" rectangle (A3)

(1) 7" x 5" rectangle (B2, C3)

From the green fabrics, cut:

(1) 4" x 9" rectangle (A2)

(1) 5½" x 13½" rectangle (B1)

(1) 4½" x 13" rectangle (C2)

(1) 5½" x 11½" rectangle (C5)

From the black text fabric, cut:

(1) 2" x 9½" strip (A1)

(1) 2" x 14½" strip (C1)

(1) 2" x 15½" strip (C4)

NEGATIVE SPACE BLOCK

FINISHED BLOCK SIZE: VARIOUS • **NUMBER OF BLOCKS: 8**

CUTTING

From the background fabric, cut:

(2) 20½" x 8½" rectangles

(1) 20½" x 12½" rectangle

(5) 10½" squares

ASSEMBLING THE QUILT TOP

1. Referring to Figure 1, arrange your blocks on your design wall.

2. Starting at the upper-left corner, stitch together the blocks to form the first row. Press the seams to the right in this row and all subsequent odd numbered rows. Press the seams of the even number rows to the left.

3. Sew the rows together. Press.

FINISHING

1. Layer with batting and backing fabric, baste, and quilt as desired.

2. Attach the binding using your favorite method.

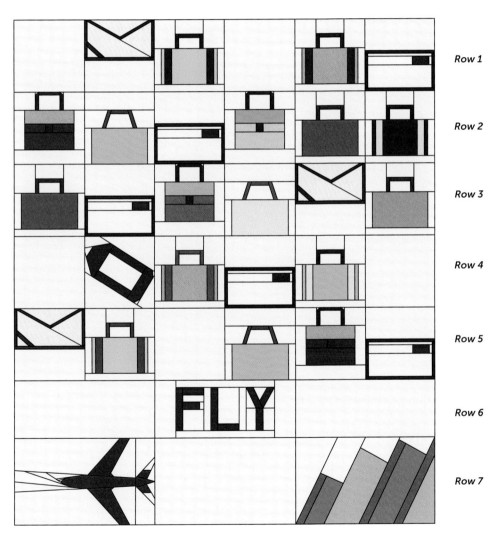

Row 1

Row 2

Row 3

Row 4

Row 5

Row 6

Row 7

Figure 1

·BRIXEN·
KREUZGASSE №130

Pictorial
Paper-Pieced
Blocks

FINISHED SIZE: 10" SQUARE

Each of these pictorial paper-pieced blocks is designed to encourage intentional piecing. In addition to lots of opportunities for fussy cutting, the designs can be enhanced by fabric selections with a suggestion of texture. These blocks also illustrate successful background fabric choices: fabrics that can be cut and seamed and still feel unified and whole. With each fabric choice you make, you are expressing your own creativity and personality and will make the block your own. Because of this, no cutting instructions are given. Follow the Finished Block images for guidance.

The blocks can be incorporated into any project that you wish. You could create pillow covers, mini quilts, a sampler, etc. Following the block instructions, there is a tote project designed with these blocks in mind. Any of the blocks can be used to customize your tote.

> Have a fabric that may make a good background but don't want to cut it up? Fold it upon itself a number of times. Does it looks choppy or uniform?

GENERAL INSTRUCTIONS FOR PAPER-PIECED BLOCKS

1. Make copies of your foundation pattern (see pages 139-154).
You can use copy paper or specialty paper made for foundation piecing.

2. Paper piece all sections and trim to include the ¼" seam allowance. Sew the sections together in the order recommended for that particular block design.

TEACHER'S PET

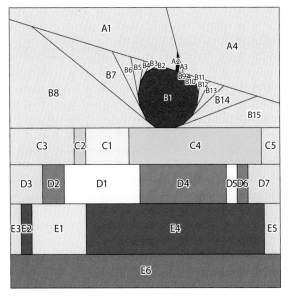

Block Diagram Teacher's Pet

Finished Block

Spines of books are so interesting and varied that finding fabrics to decorate the spines of your paper-pieced books is always an adventure. You can decide if you prefer whimsy or realism. You could add names from selvages as an author's name for piece D5, for example. Text prints and label prints are a great resource. You can also fussy cut medallion-like designs from prints. Here, a woodgrain was used to suggest the table surface. A crosshatch design in the background fabric can be distracting if there is a lot of contrast between the colors, such as a black on white crosshatch. But here, the light gray is close enough to the white that it reads as a solid and doesn't draw the eye away from the focal point of the block:the books and apple.

piecing
Sew Section A to B to C to D to E.

PENCIL CAN

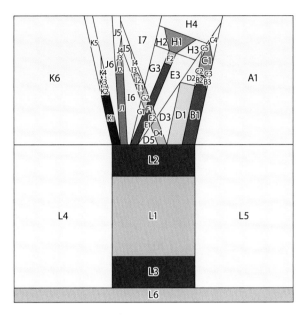

Block Diagram Pencil Can

Finished Block

Every home has an old soup can full of pencils, brushes, etc. right? I know mine does. In this block, there is an opportunity to use woodgrain for brush handles or you can make them colorful to mimic the plastic ones. A stripe gives the impression of bristles for the tip of your brush. The pencils with their coordinating leads can be colorful, prints, or your basic No. 2 pencil. The soup can label is a great spot for a fussy cut. I decided to make this a can of corn and used a quirky corn label paired with a mottled gray for the can. The background print is directional and therefore best to keep properly oriented, but since it is tone on tone, slightly imperfect alignment isn't noticeable.

piecing

1. Sew Section B to C to D to A.

2. Sew Section E to F to G to H.

3. Sew Section I to J to K.

4. Join these 3 sections together, then attach Section L.

INKWELL

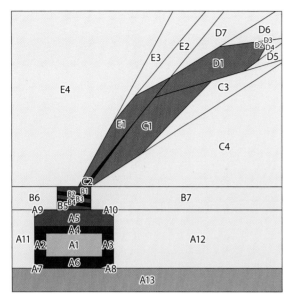

Block Diagram Inkwell

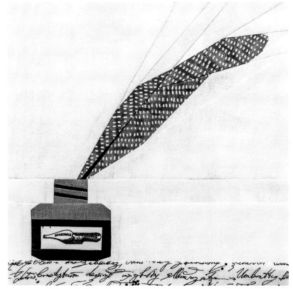

Finished Block

This inkwell block features a glass inkwell and a feather pen, giving you the opportunity to use just a touch of that perfect pen and ink script from your stash. Use a simple textured solid in the background so the feather and inkwell take center stage. The print for the feather gives a hint of texture and it is also directional. You can use that to your benefit and place the fabric so that the lines move out from the shaft at opposing diagonals. Shift the direction of the print once again for the top of the feather to suggest a turn in direction. Two shades of blue in the inkwell suggest a blue glass with darker blue ink. The label on the inkwell could be a color name, which are easily found in text prints, a company name from a label, or something like the nib I used here.

piecing

1. Sew Section A to B.

2. Sew Section C to D to E.

3. Join these 2 sections to complete the block.

BUD VASE ON DOILY

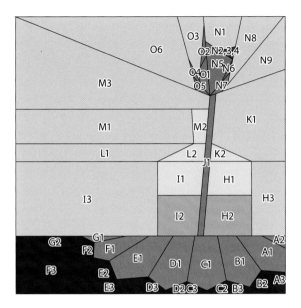

Block Diagram Bud Vase

Finished Block

A lot can be accomplished in this block using intentional color placement. Choosing translucent shades for the glass and the water give the impression of a vase half full of water. The bud itself is all cut from an ombré pink print. Choose the lightest portions of the fabric for pieces O1 and N5, the main body of the rose bud, and progressively darker shades for N4, N3, and N2, respectively. Using a single ombré cut of fabric makes cutting a cinch, but you could also create your own gradient using four separate solids. Choosing lace print fabric creates the doily look especially if you can match the lace print's background color to the surface solid. The non-directional, subtle text print makes for a successful background. The prints don't need to match from section to section and the seams disappear.

piecing

1. Sew Section A to B to C to D to E to F to G.

2. Sew Section I to L to M.

3. Sew Section K to H to J.

4. Join ILM to KHJ and then to ABCDEFG.

5. Sew Section O to N and then sew this section to the remainder of the block. It is a gentle Y seam. Simply sew to the intersection with the stem, put your needle down, pivot your fabric, and stitch to the end. There is no need to remove your foundation papers first. Press the Y seam down.

DRESS

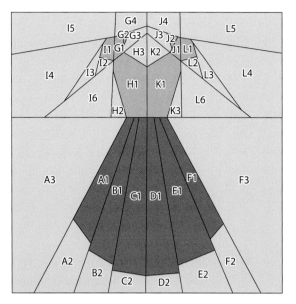

Block Diagram Dress

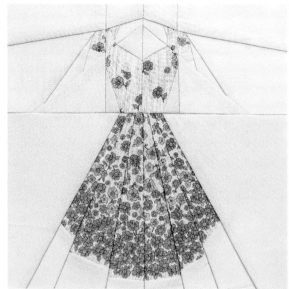

Finished Block

Sometimes a solid is the perfect choice for the background of a paper-pieced block. I chose to use one here to let the piecing in the dress really shine. Showcase the stunning effect of using a border print to piece this dress block. Use the densely printed part of the fabric, closest to the selvage, for the pieces of the skirt, arranging the densest area of floral to land at the hemline with the density decreasing toward the waist. Then use the least densely printed body of the fabric for the bodice and sleeves of the dress. Unprinted sections are used for the details along the neckline so that they wouldn't look chopped up or busy.

piecing

1. Sew Section A to B to C to D to E to F.

2. Sew Section H to G to I.

3. Sew Section K to J to L.

4. Join HGI and KJL.

5. Join bodice section to skirt section along the horizontal seam at the waistline.

BUSINESS CASUAL

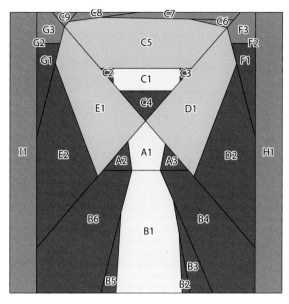

Block Diagram Business Casual

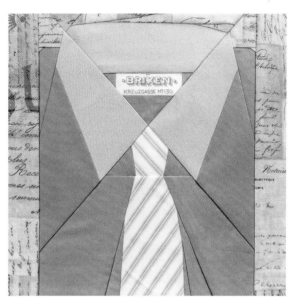

Finished Block

This simple shirt and tie block can really be enhanced by just two perfectly chosen fabrics. The shirt has a label at the back collar, which is a great place to use a text print. You might find something that works from fabric printed with labels. Remember, if your text doesn't fit exactly into the space provided by Section C1, you can adjust those straight lines surrounding that section just a touch to accommodate your fussy cut. The second fabric choice that plays a huge role in the success of this block is the tie fabric. The classic tie tends to have a diagonal stripe. Even though my print had the stripe printed along the grain of the fabric, I simply turned it for both the knot and the body of the tie to achieve the diagonal stripe. I recommend a solid for the shirt simply because it is broken by seam lines. Properly aligning a stripe or plaid would be nearly impossible, and if improperly aligned, it would be busy and detract from the overall look.

piecing

1. Sew Section A to B to D to F to H.

2. Sew Section E to G to C.

3. Join these 2 sections and add on Section I.

ACCORDION

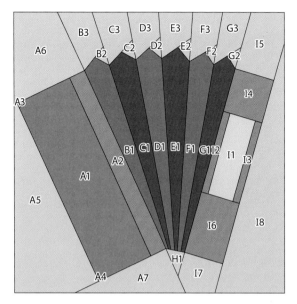

Block Diagram Accordion

Finished Block

The accordion block is a lot of fun to sew. You will feel accomplished when piecing that black-and-white stripe for piece A1 to suggest the piano-like keyboard. Think about all the piecing time you just saved! The accordion itself can be just about any color, so find your dot print first for piece I1. You want a dot that will give the impression of buttons for the button board. Once you find an evenly spaced dot that works, match the accordion body color to that print. The pleats of the bellows can alternate between lighter and darker shades to create dimension. There are so many musical notation prints out there for the background. They aren't the easiest prints to use as a background because they are directional, but if you follow my tips for paper piecing with directional fabric (see page 16), it is doable in this block.

piecing

1. Sew Section B to C to D to E to F to G and then to H.

2. Add Section I, then Section A.

CUCKOO CLOCK

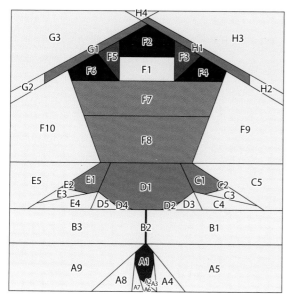

Block Diagram Cuckoo Clock

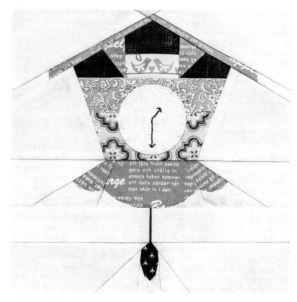

Finished Block

The Cuckoo Clock block is a chance to play with patterns and colors because these clocks are known for their charming color combinations. Choose the bird print first and let those colors guide you in your other fabric selections. If you can't find a fabric to fussy cut that fits well in piece F1, adjust your pattern piece by adding a section to the right and left of a single bird or add height to the door by raising the stitching line, joining F1 to F2.

A textured solid works well with potentially choppy seams. It keeps the background from competing with the clock but still adds dimension. I found a brown print with just enough texture to suggest the scales of a pinecone for the pendulum.

piecing

1. Sew Section A to B.

2. Sew Section C to D to E.

3. Join Sections AB and CDE to complete the lower half of the block.

4. Sew Section F to G to H to create the top half of the block.

5. Join the two halves together to complete the block.

To appliqué a clock face, cut a 3″ square of fabric and HeatnBond Lite fusible adhesive. Fuse the adhesive to the back. Cut a 2½″ circle and remove the paper. Fold the circle in quarters and crease to find the center point. Lightly draw clock hands and backstitch along those lines, using floss. Remove the papers from the back of your block. Fuse the clock face to the center of the clock front. Use a tight zigzag stitch (Fig. 1) to finish the edge of your appliqué.

Figure 1

LAUNDRY TUB

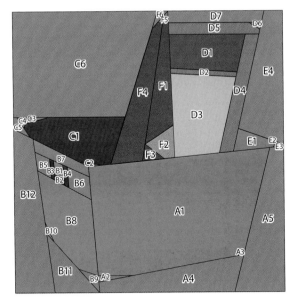

Block Diagram Laundry Tub

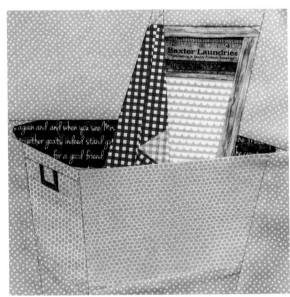

Finished Block

The laundry tub block is a fussy cutting treat! There are so many ways to enhance the design through fabric selection. The focal point of the block is the washboard. Often, washtubs would feature advertisements in piece D1, so have fun finding the perfect print. For piece D3, a scallop print suggests the rippled glass surface and gingham for the cloth hanging over the board seemed to evoke the right time period. Using the wrong side of the fabric to piece F2 makes it look like the fabric is folded back. A bit of metallic suggests a stainless steel washtub. The background fabric here is a small, irregularly shaped and placed dot, which means that the seams virtually disappear.

piecing

1. Sew Section A to B.

2. Sew Section C to F to D to E.

3. When you join the two halves of the block, you will note a very gentle Y seam. All you need to do is stitch until you come to the corner of the washtub, put your needle down, pivot, and rearrange your fabric then continue to stitch. There is no need to remove the foundation papers first. Press the center seam down.

OWL

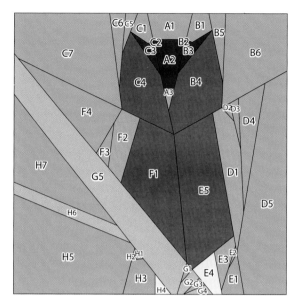

Block Diagram Owl

Finished Block

Owl feathers have so many shades and textures that you'll enjoy the different outcomes you can achieve when choosing fabric for this block. I used a tone-on-tone text print with broad painterly swaths that gives the illusion of fluffy feathers for the body. The wings are actually a woodgrain! Select fabrics that suggest feathers without being an actual feather print. The tree branch has organic lines that suggest the patterns found on bark.

piecing

1. Sew Section A to B to C.

2. Sew Section E to D to F.

3. Sew Section H to G.

4. Join HG with EDF.

5. When you join the two halves of the block, there is a gentle Y seam. Simply stitch until you come to the center of the neck seam, put your needle down, pivot, and rearrange your fabric then continue to stitch. There is no need to remove the foundation papers. Press these seams down.

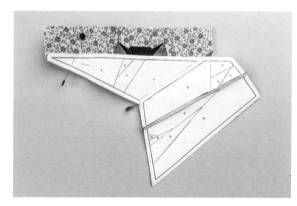

Completed Y-Seam

Stash Happy
Tote

FINISHED TOTE SIZE: 14½" x 15½" x 3"

This tote bag can be made using any of the 10" finished paper-pieced blocks from this section as the outer pocket. The fabric can be adapted to the block design and the intended use. Perhaps you will make a bag for carrying sheet music with the Accordion block, or a bag to hold your sketchbook with the Pencil Can block. You need only three half yards and a fat quarter, to make the main body of this bag— totally stash friendly! If you have these materials on hand, this project will be a quick one to make!

MATERIALS

- **(1) 10 ½" unfinished square paper-pieced block**
- **Exterior main fabric:** ½ yard
- **Contrasting binding fabric:** (1) 10½" x 2½" strip
- **Exterior side panel fabric:** ½ yard
- **Lining fabric:** ½ yard
- **Strap fabric:** fat quarter
- **HeatnBond high-loft fusible fleece:** ½ yard
- **Water-soluble pen**

CUTTING

From exterior main fabric, cut:
- (1) 10½" square for pocket lining
- (1) 10½" x 14" rectangle
- (1) 10½" x 4½" rectangle
- (1) 10½" x 18" rectangle

From exterior side panel fabric, cut:
- (4) 4½" x 18" rectangles

From fusible fleece, cut:
- (1) 10½" square
- (2) 18½" x 18" rectangles
- (2) ⅞" x 18" strips

From strap fabric, cut:
- (2) 4" x 18" strips

From lining fabric, cut:
- (2) 18½" x 18" rectangles

MAKING THE POCKET

Seam allowances are ¼''
unless otherwise stated.

1. Fuse the 10½'' square of
fusible fleece to the wrong
side of the paper-pieced
block. Position the 10½''
square of exterior main fabric
and the paper-pieced block
with right sides together
(RST). Sew along the top
edge. Position the fabrics
wrong sides together (WST)
and press.

2. Fold the binding strip in
half along the length, wrong
sides together and press.

3. Pin the strip on the top of
the stitched pocket aligning
the raw edge with the top
of the sewn pocket seam
(Fig. 1). Sew through all the
layers. Press the binding away
from the block. Bring the
folded edge to the back and
whipstitch on the lining.

Figure 1

ASSEMBLING THE PANELS

1. Position the pocket on the right side of the 10½'' x 14''
exterior main rectangle, aligning the raw edges on the bottom.
Position the 10½'' x 4½'' exterior main rectangle right side
down, pin the layers together (Fig. 2) and stitch. Press the sewn
seam open.

2. Pin and sew a 4½'' x 18'' exterior side panel to either side
of the assembled pocket panel, RST (Fig. 3). Press side seams
open and fuse the 18½'' x 18'' rectangle of fusible to the wrong
side. Edgestitch along the seams where the side panels and
assembled pocket panel meet (Fig. 4). This is the front panel.
Repeat for the remaining exterior pieces, and rectangle of
fusible to create the back panel.

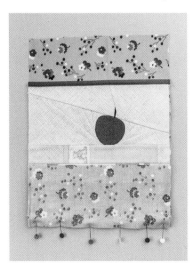

Figure 2

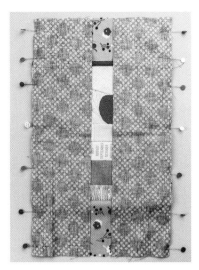

Figure 3

3. Position the fused front
and back panel RST. Stitch
along the sides and the bottom,
using a ½'' seam allowance,
backstitching at both ends of
the seam. Set aside.

4. Repeat Step 3 with the 2
lining pieces leaving a 5''
opening at the bottom for
turning.

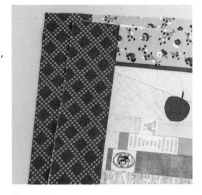

Figure 4

BOXING THE CORNERS

1. Pinch a sewn corner of the lining, carefully nesting the bottom and side seams to form a triangle and cut a horizontal line 1½" from the tip (Fig. 5). Stitch ¼" away from the cut line, backstitching at both ends.

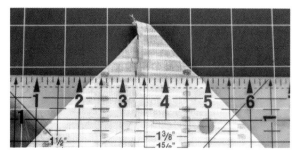

Figure 5

2. Repeat on the opposite corner of the lining and on both corners of the bag exterior.

MAKING THE STRAPS

1. Press one strap fabric strip in half along the length, WST to create a crease. Open the center fold and align the raw edges to meet at the center crease. Carefully, press along the length of the strip. Refold the strap along the original crease (enclosing the raw edges) to create a strap that is 1" wide. Insert a ⅞" x 18" strip of fusible fleece into the fold and fuse into place. Topstitch along both long edges of the strap. Repeat for the second strap. (Fig. 6)

Figure 6

2. On the right side of the front panel, use a water-soluble pen to mark 1½" away from each side seam on the pocket panel at the raw edge.

3. Position one end of the strap on the front panel, aligning the raw edges and the outside edge of the strap with the mark from Step 2.

4. Repeat for the other side of the strap, ensuring that the strap does not twist. Pin (Fig. 7) and baste the strap into place using a ⅛" seam allowance.

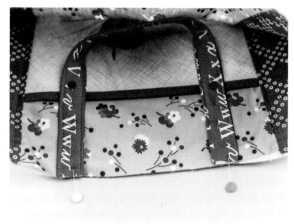

Figure 7

5. Repeat Steps 3 and 4 to attach the second strap to the back panel.

6. Insert the main bag into the lining, RST. Match seams, pin, and stitch around the upper edge, using a ½" seam allowance.

7. Turn the bag through the opening and press the top of the bag carefully so that the lining does not show. Topstitch along the upper edge of the bag.

8. Hand stitch the opening in the lining closed.

Tumble 'Round Quilt

FINISHED BLOCK SIZE: 8″ SQUARE • **FINISHED SIZE: 64″ x 64″**

NUMBER OF BLOCKS: 64

This quilt demonstrates how the thoughtful fabric placement of a single, carefully selected directional print can add dramatic movement to a quilt. It is a little tricky to find prints that are not only directional — meaning that they are oriented in a certain direction — but that also have a direction that suggests motion. That's what I was looking for here.

MATERIALS

- **Solid background fabric:** 2½ yards
- **Near-solid tone-on-tone background fabric:** 1 yard
- **Directional print:** approximately 1½ yards
- **Orange print for blades:** 1¼ yards
- **Cream print for blades:** 1¼ yards
- **Inner band print for Section A3:** 1 yard
- **Center solid:** ⅓ yard
- **Backing fabric:** 4 yards
- **Binding fabric:** ½ yard
- **Batting:** 70″ x 70″

intentional piecing

I searched for the perfect print and ultimately chose a print in which aloe plants point in one direction. The directional print is placed facing in one direction in half of the blocks and in the opposing direction in the other half. The blocks are then arranged so that alternating rows of the quilt appear to spin in opposite directions. In order to add more motion to the quilt, the placement of the cream and orange prints are also reversed in alternating rows.

NOTE:

When cutting your directional band for Section B1, begin by holding the fabric to the wrong side of your foundation pattern. Hold it against a window or other light source to make sure that the print works with the width of the pattern piece. Decide what portion of the print you want to center on the band. In this example, I wanted to center two rows of aloe. I focused less on the 3½''-wide cutting suggestion and more on the fabric print. Use your own judgment based on the print you have chosen. Keep in mind that sometimes the design isn't printed completely straight on the fabric, so you do not want to simply cut 3½'' strips by the WOF. I lined my ruler up with the center of the aloe and cut (Fig. 1). I skipped over two rows of aloe and cut along the center of the next aloe.

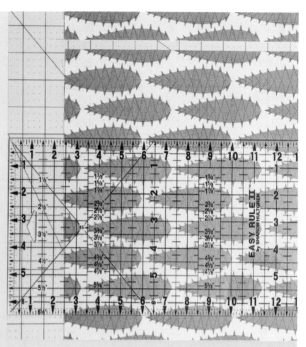

Figure 1

CUTTING

WOF = width of fabric

From solid background fabric, cut:
(24) 11'' squares
subcut each square
on the diagonal

From near-solid background fabric, cut:
(8) 11'' squares
subcut each square
on the diagonal

From directional print, cut:
(13) approximately
3½'' x WOF fussy cut strips

From orange blade print, cut:
(11) 3½'' x WOF strips

From cream blade print, cut:
(11) 3½'' x WOF strips

From inner band print, cut:
(10) 3½'' x WOF strips

From center solid, cut:
(32) 3'' squares
subcut each square
on the diagonal

PREPARATION

Make 64 copies of the foundation pattern (see page 155).

ASSEMBLING THE TUMBLE 'ROUND BLOCKS

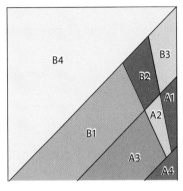

Block Diagram

Finished Block

The paper piecing process is the same as illustrated with step-by-step photographs for the Tell Me a Story Quilt on page 26. However, the sections of this block are not quite as easy to piece. My secret for piecing awkward shapes can be found in Paper Piecing Essentials (see page 12).

1. Referring to the Block Diagram above, paper piece each section of the block.

Piece 32 blocks with directional fabric pointing clockwise in Section B1

- B2 and A1 pieced with cream blade print

- B3 and A2 pieced with orange blade print

Piece the other 32 blocks with directional fabric pointing counterclockwise in Section B1

- B2 and A1 pieced with orange blade print

- B3 and A2 pieced with cream blade print

2. Position completed sections with right side down and, using your ruler, trim each block along the ¼" seam allowance as indicated on the pattern.

3. Within each set of 32 blocks, sew A sections to B sections. Press half the seams toward Section B and half toward Section A.

ASSEMBLING THE QUILT TOP

1. Group the blocks into sets of two, consulting Figure 2 and keeping the blocks with counterclockwise prints together. Similarly, group and keep together the clockwise prints. Join each pair by stitching along the seam line. Do not press the seams.

Figure 2

2. Referring to Figure 3, arrange the block pairs on your design wall. Be careful to keep the pairs in the determined order. Press the center seams in alternating directions.

3. Nest the seams and sew into rows. Press.

4. Sew the rows together to complete the quilt top.

FINISHING

1. Layer with batting and backing fabric. Baste, and quilt as desired.

2. Attach the binding using your favorite method.

I quilted this project using concentric circles, beginning with a circle on the third row down from the top, third complete block in from the left. I think that the radiating circles complement the whirling design.

Figure 3

Lucy Clutch

FINISHED SIZE: 14" x 7"

There are a number of beautiful border prints on the market. Border prints generally have a more concentrated design running along the selvage edge of the fabric. Often they are used for tablecloths or clothing, especially skirts. Recently, border prints have been showing up on linen and canvas, which are the perfect weight for bag making. If you decide to use a regular weight quilting cotton, be sure to fuse a layer of lightweight interfacing to the wrong side for increased durability.

MATERIALS

- **Exterior fabric:** ½ yard
- **Lining fabric:** 1 fat quarter
- **HeatnBond non-woven craft fusible interfacing**
- **Magnetic snap**

intentional piecing

This envelope-style clutch was designed to highlight such a border print. The exterior flap is cut along the selvage edge of the border print, and the rest of the bag is cut avoiding the border. The large, flat, envelope-style of this clutch harkens back to the 1950s, but the fabric is very much today and provides added interest.

CUTTING

From exterior fabric, cut:
2 Body Patterns (see page 156) on the fold

1 Flap Pattern (see page 157) with angle placed flush with the edge of the fabric, just beside the selvage

From lining fabric, cut:
2 Body Patterns on the fold

1 mirror image of Flap Pattern

From interfacing, cut:
2 Body Patterns on the fold

1 Flap Template

ASSEMBLING THE BAG

Seam allowances are ¼'' unless otherwise stated.

1. Place the lining flap piece onto one lining bag piece, right sides together, aligning upper raw edges. Stitch along upper edge and set aside (Fig. 1). This is the back lining.

2. Place the fused exterior flap piece onto one fused exterior bag piece, right sides together, aligning the upper raw edges. Stitch along the upper edge and set aside (Fig. 2). This is the back exterior.

3. Place the remaining lining bag piece onto the remaining fused exterior bag piece, right sides together. Stitch along the upper edge (Fig. 3). This unit is the bag front.

Figure 1

Figure 2

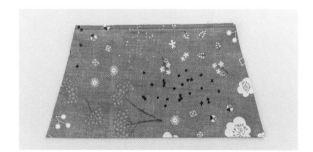

Figure 3

4. Position body fabrics wrong sides together. Press at the top seams, pressing seams away from the flap for both back pieces, and edgestitch along all three pieces. (Figs. 4-6)

5. Position the lining piece right side up on the table. Next, place the bag front (right side up) on top and pin along the raw edges. Following the manufacturer's directions, install the male side of a magnetic snap on the flap lining at the point indicated on the template. Make sure it is at least ½'' in from all edges. Fold the flap over to mark the location of the female side of the snap. Install it in the exterior fabric layer only. (Fig. 7)

6. Baste the bag front to the lining about ⅛'' from the raw edges along both sides and the bottom.

7. Place the exterior body and flap unit on top of this unit, right sides together. Pin. Stitch around the perimeter leaving an opening of about 3'' for turning on the long side of the flap, backstitching at each end. (Fig. 8)

8. Clip corners and turn right side out. Carefully turn under the raw edges of the opening and press. Edgestitch around the flap, securing stitches at both ends. Be careful as you approach the snap that it doesn't bump your presser foot and cause uneven stitching.

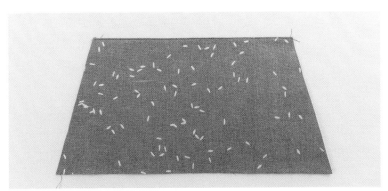

Figure 4

Figure 5

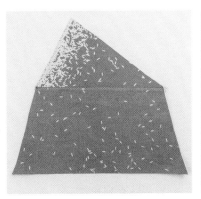

Figure 6

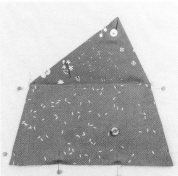

Figure 7

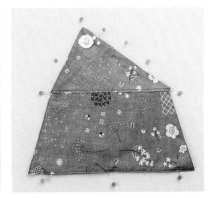

Figure 8

Crazy Eights Quilt

FINISHED BLOCK SIZE: **16" SQUARE** • FINISHED QUILT SIZE: **64" x 64"**

NUMBER OF BLOCKS: **16**

I solemnly vow to never underestimate the power of a striped fabric again. I have never stashed them or sought them out. Now I am wondering why. They hold the power of a carefully, precisely strip-pieced section with zero effort. In this quilt design, I hope to illustrate the wonder of stripes and get them into your quilt tops rather than just the bindings!

MATERIALS

The yardage requirements are somewhat variable. It will depend on the width of your stripe and how many sections you choose to piece with each stripe. For this example, I used approximately:

- **Wide (1") striped fabric:** 1/2 yard

- **Medium (1/2"–3/4") striped fabrics:** 1/2 yard each of 5 fabrics

- **Medium (1/2"–3/4") striped fabrics:** fat quarter each of 3 fabrics

- **Narrow (1/4" or narrower) striped fabrics:** fat quarter each of 2 fabrics

- **Narrow (1/4" or narrower) striped fabrics:** 1/2 yard each of 2 fabrics

- **Narrow (1/4" or narrower) striped fabric (to be used at an alternate angle):** 1/2 yard

- **Background fabric:** 5 yards

- **Batting:** 70" x 70"

- **Backing fabric:** 4 yards

- **Binding fabric:** 1/2 yard

- **20-lb. copy paper**

> My advice is to buy a couple of extra striped fabrics. The cutting is a bit wasteful, though I prefer not to think of it that way. If it yields the results you are looking for, then it is an investment in your design!

NOTE:

When cutting the template pieces from the striped fabrics, cut about ½" beyond all seam allowances for ease of piecing.

CUTTING

WOF = width of fabric

From striped fabrics, cut:

(32) pieces from a variety of stripes using Section A1 as a template

(32) pieces from a variety of stripes using Section B1 as a template

(32) pieces from a variety of stripes using Section C1 as a template

(16) pieces from a variety of stripes using Section D1 as a template

(16) pieces from the narrow striped fabric to be used at an alternate angle using Section D1 as a template

From background fabric, cut:

(64) 5" x 10½" rectangles

(11) 8" x WOF strips

intentional piecing

There is a trick that makes this an easy pattern to piece. Find stripes in a variety of widths. Striped fabrics typically come with ½", ¾," and 1" spacing, but you can find stripes that are irregularly spaced as well. If you carefully place your fabrics so that stripes of different spacing intersect along seam lines, you avoid having to precisely match stripes along the bias seams. I was able to find stripes that included text and numbers, which provide added interest.

PREPARATION

Make 32 copies of the foundation patterns A-D (see pages 158-159).

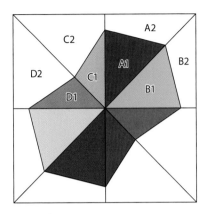

Block Diagram

Finished Block

ASSEMBLING THE BLOCK

1. Reference the Finished Block photograph above for placement of the wide, medium and narrow striped fabrics.

2. Assemble all A and B sections. To piece the striped A1 and B1 sections, hold the pattern and striped fabric, with wrong sides together, to the light. Line up the outer edge of one colored stripe with the stitching line between Section A1 and A2 or B1 and B2. Pin. Then place your background fabric and the striped fabrics right sides together and stitch your seam. Using your ruler, trim the seam allowances to ¼'' and press.

3. Assemble all C sections and 16 of the D sections in the same manner.

4. Piece 16 of the D1 sections using the narrow stripe set aside for piecing at an alternate angle. Rather than arranging the stripe along the seam line between D1 and D2, place the colored stripe flush with the outer block seam line. Using your ruler, trim the seam allowances to ¼'' and press.

5. Position all pieced sections with right sides down. Trim the seam allowances to ¼''.

6. Randomly sew A sections to B sections along the diagonal, varying the pairing of your stripes.

7. Randomly sew C sections to D sections along the diagonal, varying the pairing of your stripes.

8. Join AB sections to CD sections. Press all seams toward Section CD.

9. Group these block halves into blocks, taking care to use one alternately pieced Section D1 per group. Press the seams in opposite directions. Nest the seams and sew the halves together.

ASSEMBLING THE QUILT TOP

1. Referring to Figure 1, arrange the blocks in a 4 by 4 layout. Starting at the upper-left corner, stitch the blocks together to form the first row. Press the seams to the right in this row and all subsequent odd numbered rows. Press the seams of the even number rows to the left.

2. Sew the rows together. Press.

FINISHING

1. Layer with batting and backing fabric. Baste, and quilt as desired.

2. Attach the binding using your favorite method.

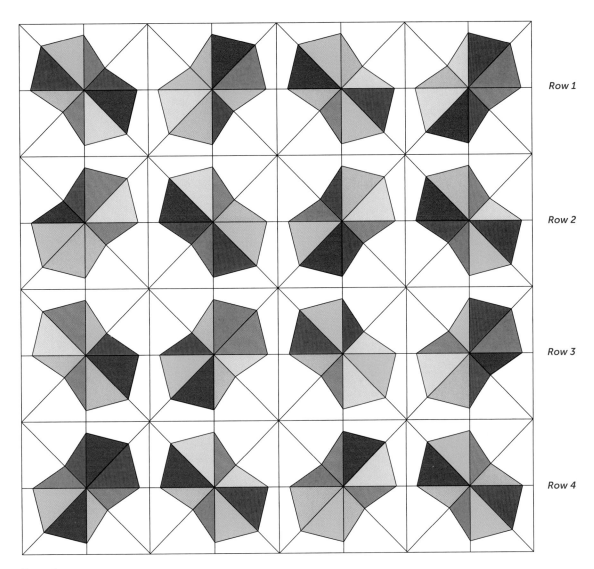

Row 1

Row 2

Row 3

Row 4

Figure 1

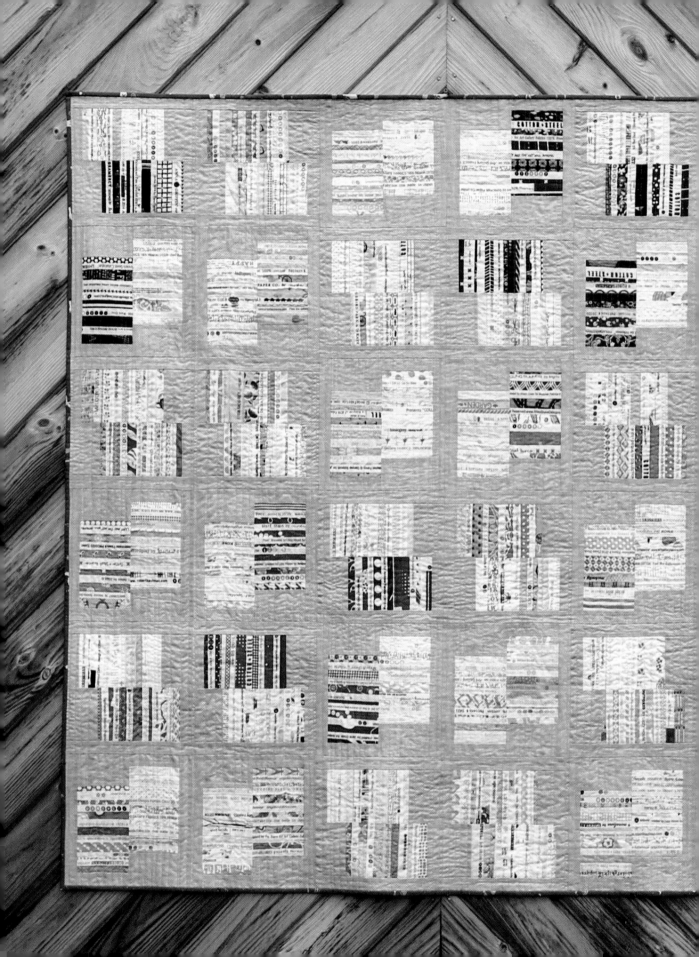

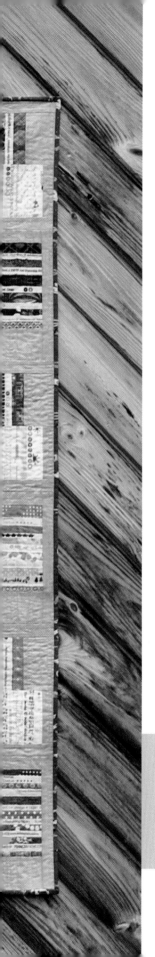

Circuitry Quilt

FINISHED BLOCK SIZE: 10" SQUARE • **FINISHED QUILT SIZE: 60" x 60"**

NUMBER OF BLOCKS: 36

In recent years, some fabric companies have begun catering to selvage collectors by using small motifs such as flowers or raindrops instead of dots on the selvage. Collecting selvages captures all your sewing memories of favorite fabrics and occasions, in one quilt. If you are starting a selvage collection, cut them to include ½" to 1" of the print beyond the selvage.

MATERIALS

- **Assorted scraps at least 1"- 1 ½" x 5":**
  36 low-volume scraps

  2 each of gray, peach, orange, chartreuse, pink, black, purple, and lavender scraps

  4 each of yellow, green, red, aqua, and navy scraps

- **Selvages:**
  assortment of low-volume selvages

  sort into piles of the following colors: gray, yellow, peach, orange, chartreuse, green, red, aqua, pink, black, navy, purple, and lavender

- **Background fabric:** 2¼ yards

- **Backing fabric:** 3¾ yards

- **Binding fabric:** ½ yard

- **Muslin foundation (optional):** 2 yards

- **Batting:** 66" x 66"

intentional piecing

Rainbow gradations are great for selvage quilt designs as are block designs that use short sections since selvages do not lie flat. Each block is composed half of hued selvages and half of low-volume selvages sewn to a foundation of muslin or paper.

NOTE:

It's nice to be able to position selvages as you work, so for this quilt, I didn't pre-cut the lengths. It is also difficult to know how many you will need until you start piecing, so cut as you go!

CUTTING

WOF = width of fabric

From assorted scraps, cut:

(36) 1″- 1½″ x 5″ low-volume strips

(2) 1″- 1½″ x 5″ each of gray, peach, orange, chartreuse, pink, black, purple, and lavender strips

(4) 1″- 1½″ x 5″ each of yellow, green, red, aqua, and navy strips

From background fabric, cut:

(3) 10½″ x WOF strips
subcut (72) 10½″ x 1½″ strips

(9) 4½″ x WOF strips
subcut (72) 1½″ x 4½″ strips

subcut (72) 3″ x 4½″ rectangles

From paper or muslin, cut:

(72) 7″ x 4½″ foundations

ASSEMBLING THE CIRCUITRY BLOCKS

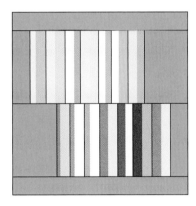

Block Diagram

Finished Block

Selvages are sewn to each other, the finished edge of one selvage overlapping the raw edge of the selvage before it. A foundation is necessary to lend stability. You can use a paper foundation and remove the paper before assembling your quilt sandwich. Or you can use muslin. It will add a bit of bulk and weight to your quilt but also warmth and stability. I used a paper foundation.

1. To begin piecing, align a 1″-1½″ x 5″ strip of fabric from a given color group along one end of a foundation piece. Remembering that you will have a ¼″ seam allowance and want at least ¼″ of the fabric to show, place the finished edge of your first selvage ½″-¾″ from the edge of the foundation. You can make sure that the selvage is straight by placing your foundation on a cutting mat and lining the selvage up with the ruler markings on either side.

2. Pin the selvage in place and then edgestitch along the finished selvage edge.

3. Trim the scrap behind the selvage to ¼″. Do not trim the raw edge of the selvage.

4. Place the finished edge of the next selvage, from the same color group, leaving about ½″ of the print showing from the selvage strip before it. Vary the placement of the strips depending on the width of your selvage and the print. If you particularly like a print, let a little more of it show. (Fig. 1)

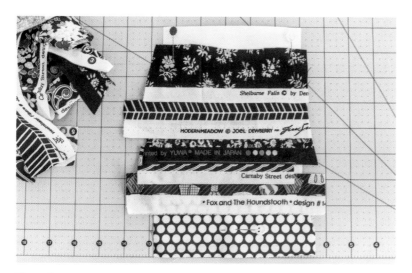

Figure 1

Sometimes you can line your next selvage up using the design of the selvage print prior. But be careful — not all designs are printed straight. You might need to split the difference between what looks straight according to the print and what the mat tells you is straight.

5. Continue until your foundation is covered. It takes approximately 6-8 selvages to complete a block.

6. Position the block with the fabric side down. Trim to the edges of the foundation. The foundation measurements include the seam allowance.

7. Repeat this process for each color until you have a total of 36 low-volume blocks; 2 blocks each of gray, peach, orange, chartreuse, pink, black, purple, and lavender; and 4 blocks each of yellow, green, red, aqua, and navy.

8. Chain piece to attach the background fabric strips. Sew the 1½″ x 4½″ strips to the end of each block where you finished piecing your selvages (not the scrap fabric end where you started). Press the fabric away from the selvage block.

9. Chain piece the 3″ x 4½″ background rectangles to the opposite ends of the selvage blocks (the ends where you started piecing with the scrap fabric). Press the fabric away from the selvage block.

10. Pair a low-volume block with a colored block so that they are off-set and stitch the center seam of the block. Press this seam open. (Fig. 2)

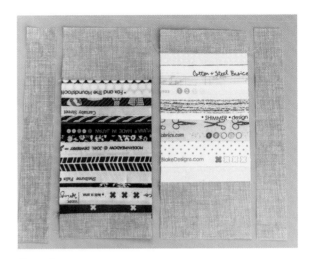

Figure 2

11. Sew the 10½″ x 1½″ background strips to the top and bottom of each block. Press away from the selvage block.

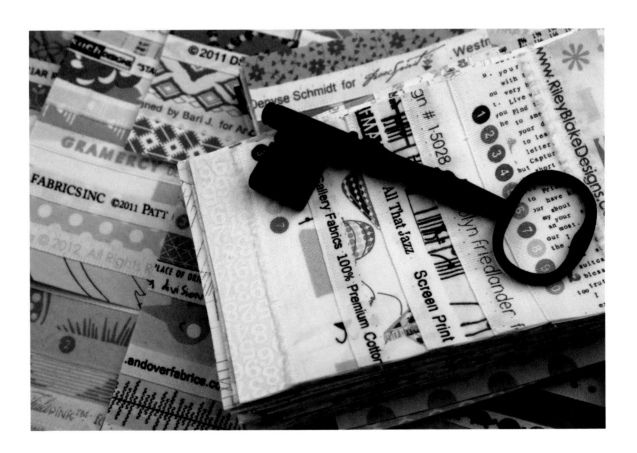

ASSEMBLING THE QUILT TOP

1. Referring to Figure 3, arrange the blocks on your design wall as shown. Starting at the upper-left corner, stitch together the blocks to form the first row. Press the seams to the right in this row and all subsequent odd numbered rows. Press the seams of the even numbered rows to the left.

2. Sew the rows together. Press.

FINISHING

1. Layer with batting and backing fabric. Baste and quilt as desired.

2. Attach the binding using your favorite method.

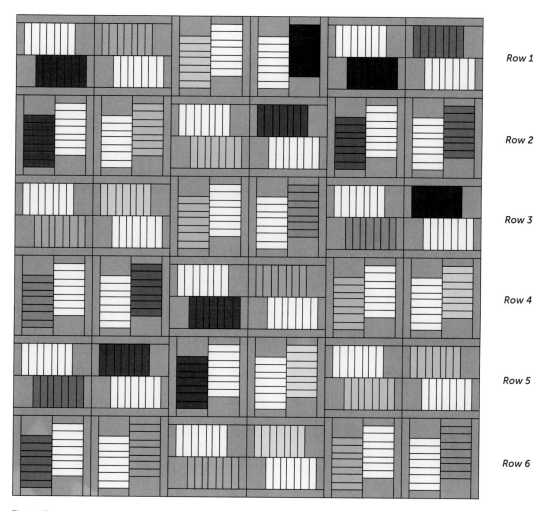

Row 1

Row 2

Row 3

Row 4

Row 5

Row 6

Figure 3

According to the dictionary,
"color ramp" is another way
to say "color gradient" —
hence the name of this quilt!

Ramp It Up
Quilt

FINISHED BLOCK SIZE: 18" SQUARE • **FINISHED QUILT SIZE:** 72" x 72"

NUMBER OF BLOCKS: 16

When I think about intentional piecing, I initially think of fussy cutting and directional prints and the topics already covered in this book. But the placement of color is very intentional too. Using a color gradient in your work is often very effective. This quilt demonstrates the powerful statement that a color gradient can make when the colors are carefully selected and purposefully placed.

It can be difficult to find solids in perfect gradations of color. Finding just three is pretty doable, so I limited this design to three shades of green. For maximum impact, choose a light, medium, and dark.

MATERIALS

- **Mint fabric:** 1½ yards
- **Medium green fabric:** 2½ yards
- **Jade green fabric:** 2 yards
- **Backing fabric:** 4½ yards
- **Binding:** ⅝ yard
- **Batting:** 80" x 80"

intentional piecing

Arranging fabrics of one color but of different values that range from light to dark or dark to light, creates a color gradient. Gradients are an intentional use of color in your piecing. Where fussy cutting focuses on highlighting the design elements in a printed fabric, color gradients emphasize the value range of a selection of solids or prints.

CUTTING

WOF = width of fabric

From mint fabric, cut:

(20) 2½″ x WOF strips

subcut (32) 2½″ squares

(32) 2½″ x 4½″ rectangles

(32) 2½″ x 6½″ rectangles

(32) 2½″ x 8½″ rectangles

From medium green fabric, cut:

(9) 8½″ x WOF strips

subcut (144) 2½″ x 8½″ rectangles

From jade green fabric, cut:

(24) 2½″ x WOF strips

subcut (32) 2½″ squares

(32) 2½″ x 4½″ rectangles

(32) 2½″ x 6½″ rectangles

(32) 2½″ x 8½″ rectangles

(16) 2½″ x 10½″ rectangles .

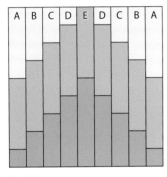

Block Diagram

ASSEMBLING THE BLOCKS

1. Sew 32 strip sets A: (1) 2½″ jade green square, to (1) 2½″ x 8½″ medium green strip, to (1) 2½″ x 8½″ mint green strip. Press the seams up in 16 sets and down in the other 16 strip sets.

2. Sew 32 strip sets B: (1) 2½″ x 4½″ jade green strip, to (1) 2½″ x 8½″ medium green strip, to (1) 2½″ x 6½″ mint green strip. Press the seams to the darker fabric.

3. Sew 32 strip sets C: (1) 2½″ x 6½″ jade green strip, to (1) 2½″ x 8½″ medium green strip, to (1) 2½″ x 4½″ mint green strip. Press the seams to the darker fabric.

4. Sew 32 strip sets D: (1) 2½″ x 8½″ jade green strip, to (1) 2½″ x 8½″ medium green strip, to (1) 2½″ mint green square. Press the seams to the darker fabric.

5. Sew 16 strip sets E: (1) 2½″ x 10½″ jade green strip, to (1) 2½″ x 8½″ medium green strip. Press seams to the darker fabric.

6. Make a block by sewing strip sets together according to the Block Diagram. Begin each block with an A seam pressed down, and end each block with an A seam pressed up. The vertical seams should be pressed to the right.

7. Repeat Step 6 to create a total of 16 blocks.

ASSEMBLING THE QUILT TOP

1. Sew together 4 blocks. The seams will nest nicely where they join. Make 4 identical rows. Press all seams to the right.

2. Referring to Figure 1, invert the second and forth row of blocks.

3. Sew the rows together. All seams should nest nicely. Press.

FINISHING

1. Layer with batting and backing fabric. Baste, and quilt as desired.

2. Attach the binding using your favorite method.

Figure 1

RESOURCES

The quirky text and Japanese prints that I gravitate toward, plus terrific textured solids and the necessary extra materials, can be found in the following shops:

Sew Me a Song
www.sewmeasong.etsy.com

Pink Castle Fabrics
www.pinkcastlefabrics.com

Super Buzzy
www.superbuzzy.com

Plastic Templates
Jo-Ann Fabrics
or your local quilting shop

Rare Earth Magnets
www.appliedmagnets.com

HeatnBond products
www.thermoweb.com

ACKNOWLEDGMENTS

I would like to thank my mother, who continues to answer the phone every time I call, even for the fourth or fifth time that day, to talk about my designs, my fabric selections, my progress, or my frustrations. Mom, you have never stopped nurturing my creativity and supporting my pursuit of my dreams. Thank you.

Thank you to my husband, who listens to me enough so that he knows the definitions of quilting terms like fussy cutting, paper piecing, and basting. I feel his presence and support every time I sit down to sew at the sewing tables he made for me or use the seam rippers he handcrafted for me.

I appreciate my children's patience while I worked on this book and will bask in their pride when they hold it in their hands.

Art Gallery Fabrics, Cotton + Steel (a division of RJR Fabrics), Moda, ThermOWeb and The Warm Company provided fabric, adhesives, and batting for many of the projects in this book. For that I am grateful.

So many people allowed me into their yards to photograph my quilts. Thank you! These include: Alpaca Naturals, John and Judy Durant, Maple Crest Farm, Plum Island Flight School, Jamus and Tara Driscoll, and Marty and Joann Lonergan. Thank you, Alyson Tedeschi, Laura Collins, John Durant, and my daughter Penny for modeling for me.

Thank you to the whole team at Lucky Spool for your combined efforts, especially Susanne Woods for her trust in me and my vision and for coming up with the most perfect title for my book.

THE
templates

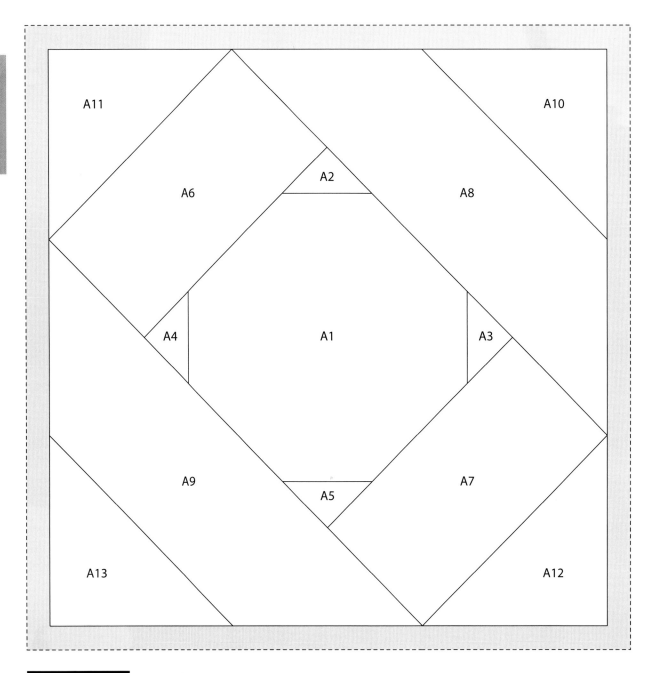

TELL ME A STORY
Block Template

Actual Size

--- cut line

—— stitch line

seam allowance

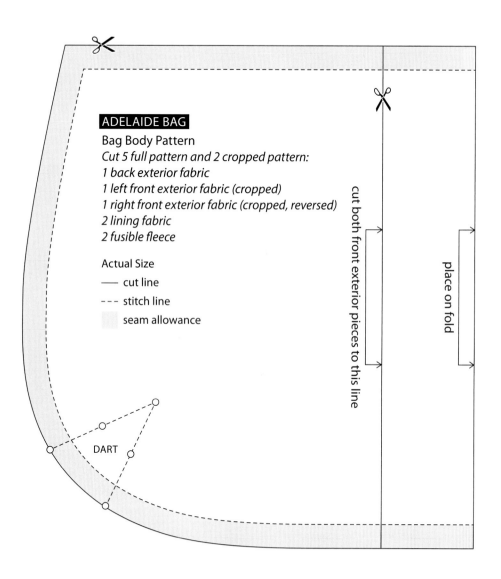

ADELAIDE BAG

Bag Body Pattern
Cut 5 full pattern and 2 cropped pattern:
1 back exterior fabric
1 left front exterior fabric (cropped)
1 right front exterior fabric (cropped, reversed)
2 lining fabric
2 fusible fleece

Actual Size

—— cut line

--- stitch line

█ seam allowance

DART

cut both front exterior pieces to this line

place on fold

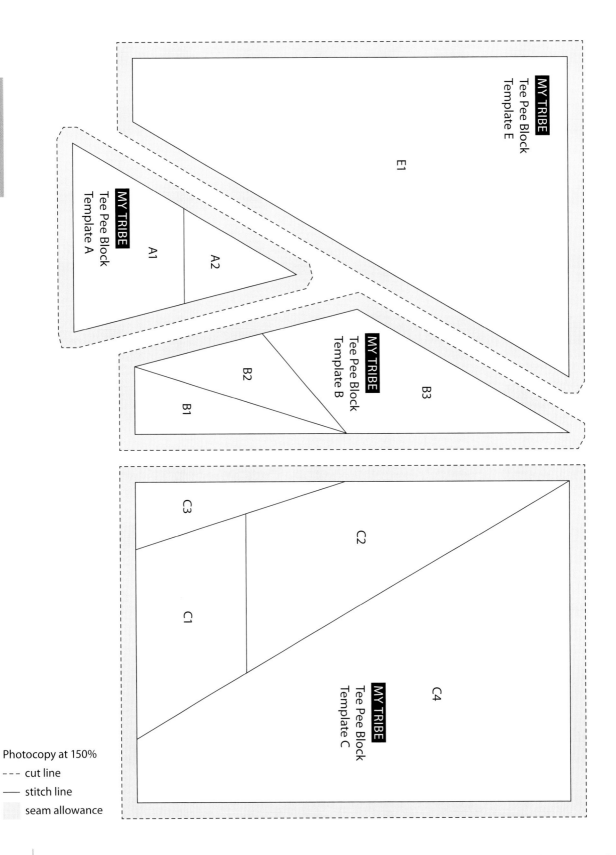

MY TRIBE
Tee Pee Block
Template E

E1

MY TRIBE
Tee Pee Block
Template A

A1

A2

MY TRIBE
Tee Pee Block
Template B

B1

B2

B3

MY TRIBE
Tee Pee Block
Template C

C1

C2

C3

C4

Photocopy at 150%

- - - cut line

——— stitch line

seam allowance

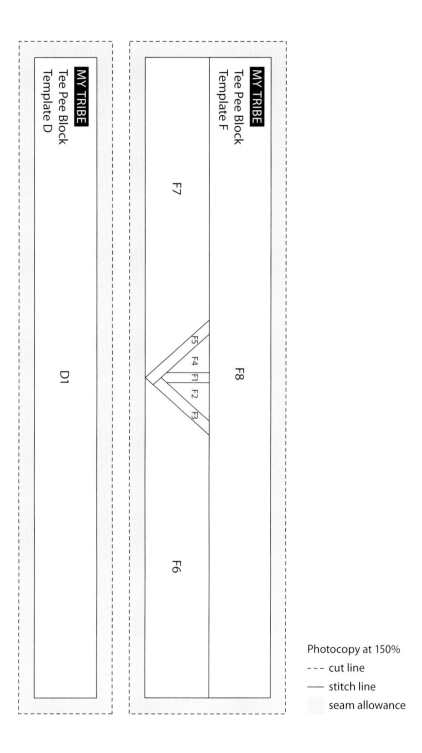

MY TRIBE
Tee Pee Block
Template F

F7

F8

F5 F4 F1 F2 F3

F6

MY TRIBE
Tee Pee Block
Template D

D1

Photocopy at 150%

--- cut line

— stitch line

seam allowance

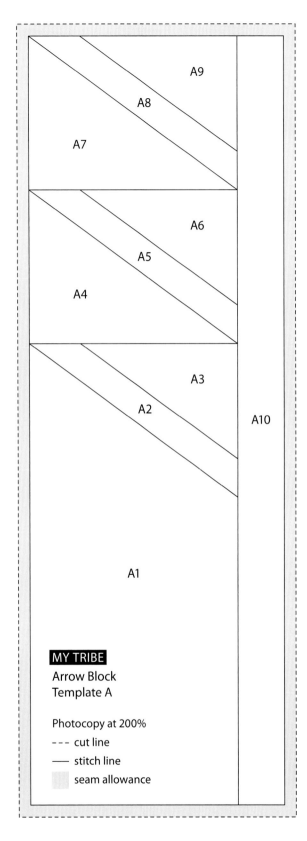

A9

A8

A7

A6

A5

A4

A3

A2

A10

A1

MY TRIBE

Arrow Block
Template A

Photocopy at 200%

--- cut line

—— stitch line

⬜ seam allowance

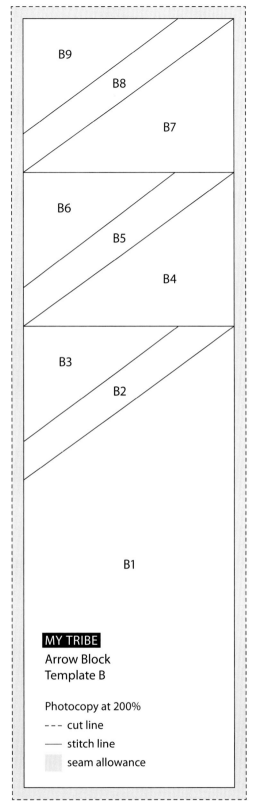

B9

B8

B7

B6

B5

B4

B3

B2

B1

MY TRIBE

Arrow Block
Template B

Photocopy at 200%

--- cut line

—— stitch line

⬜ seam allowance

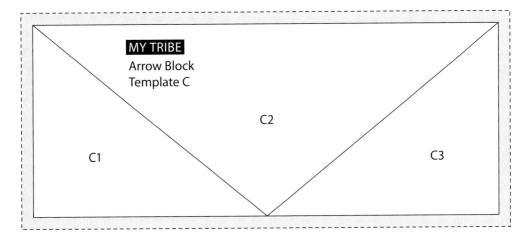

MY TRIBE
Arrow Block
Template C

C2

C1

C3

Photocopy at 200%

- - - cut line

—— stitch line

seam allowance

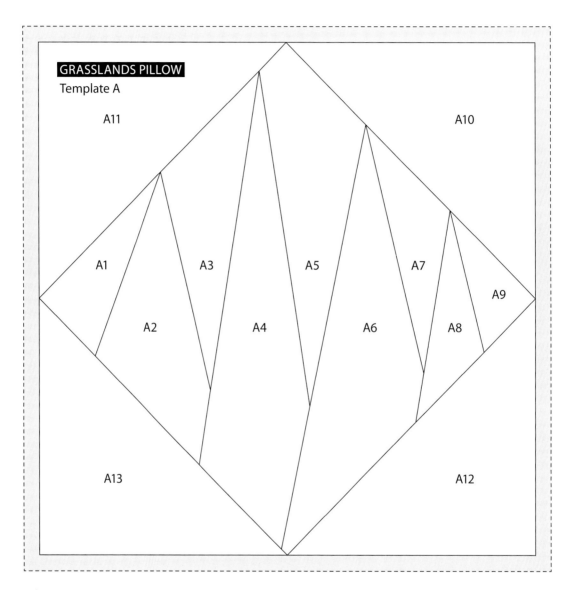

GRASSLANDS PILLOW

Template A

A11

A10

A1

A3

A5

A7

A9

A2

A4

A6

A8

A13

A12

Photocopy at 150%

- - - cut line

——— stitch line

■ seam allowance

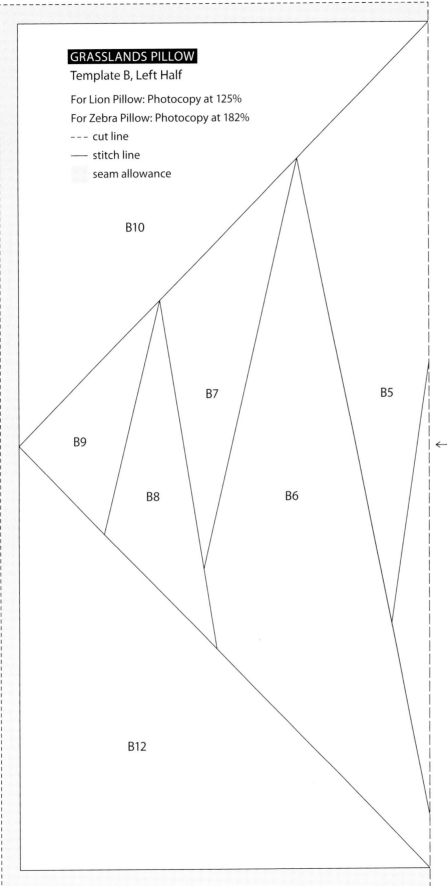

GRASSLANDS PILLOW

Template B, Left Half

For Lion Pillow: Photocopy at 125%

For Zebra Pillow: Photocopy at 182%

--- cut line

—— stitch line

seam allowance

B10

B7

B5

B9

B8

B6

B12

To make complete template: join left and right template halves at this long-dashed line

GRASSLANDS PILLOW

Template B, Right Half

For Lion Pillow: Photocopy at 125%

For Zebra Pillow: Photocopy at 182%

- - - cut line

—— stitch line

▨ seam allowance

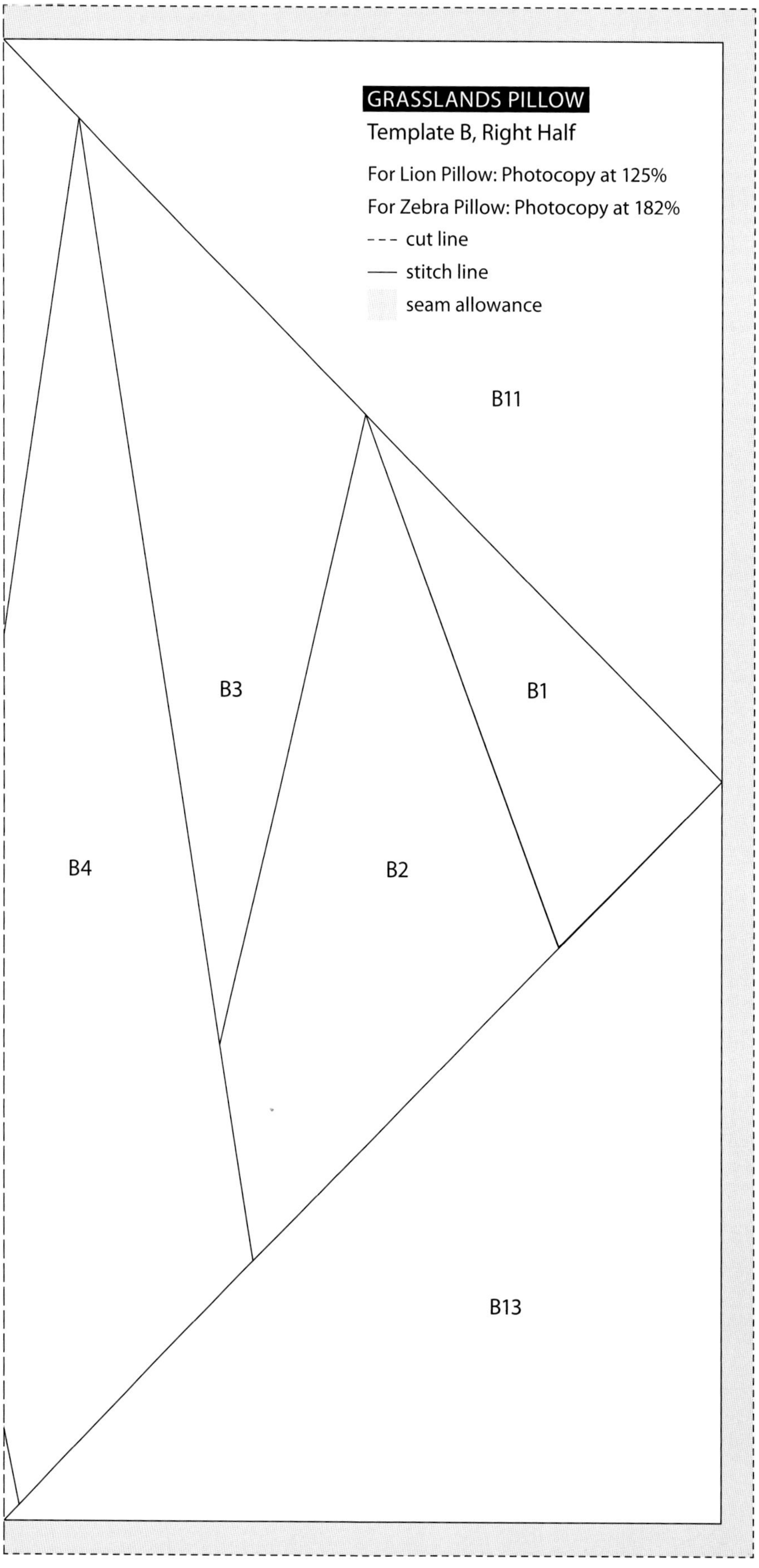

B11

B3

B1

B4

B2

B13

To make complete template: join left and right template halves at this long-dashed line

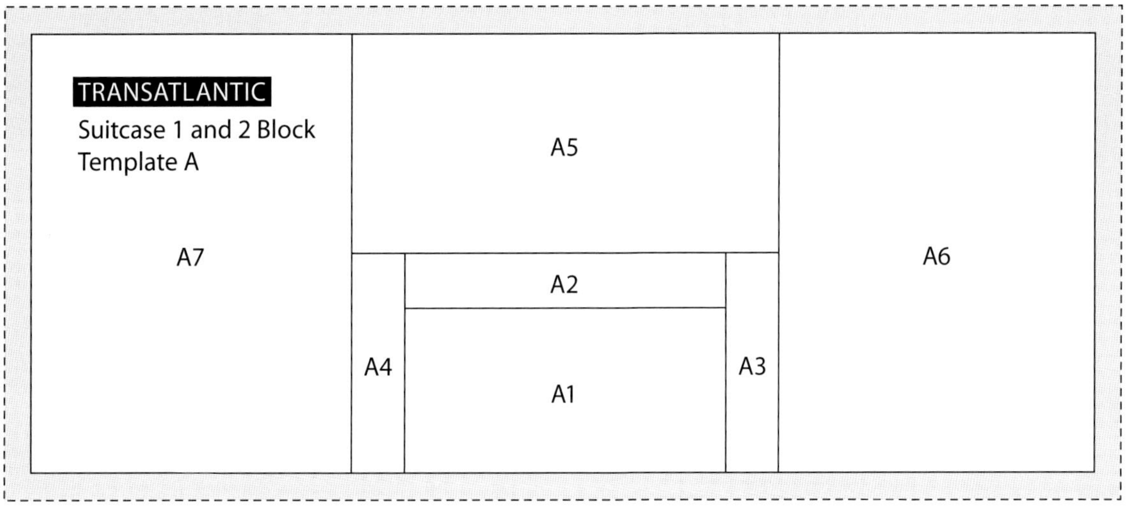

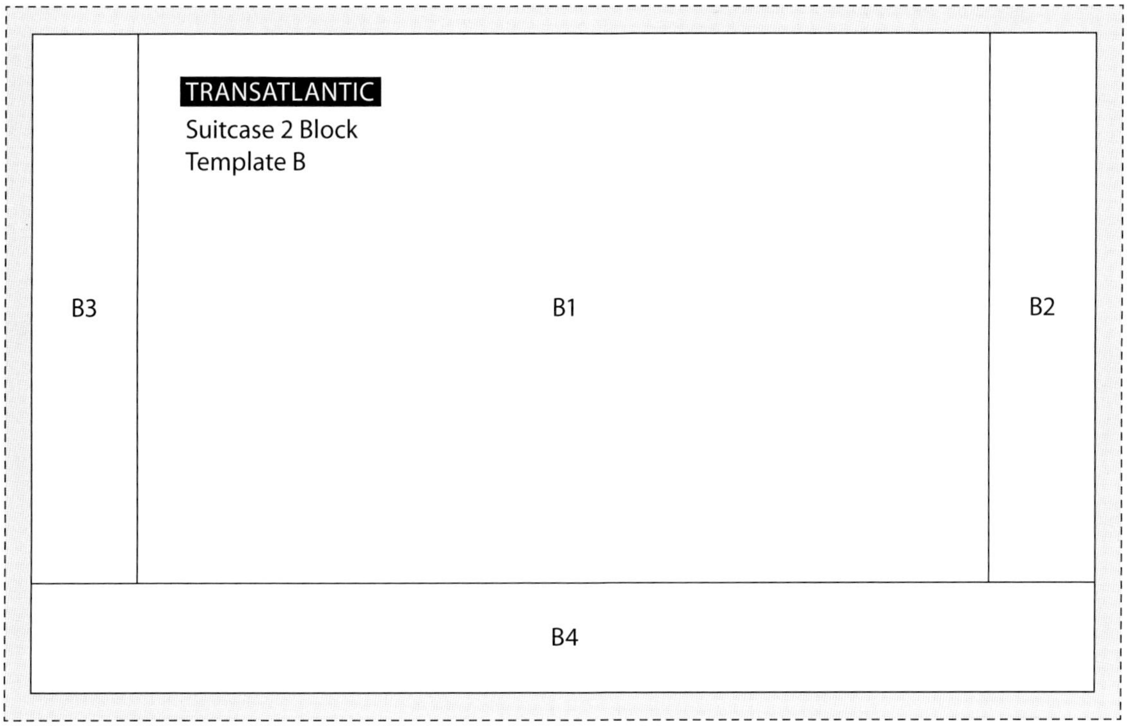

TRANSATLANTIC

Suitcase 1 and 2 Block
Template A

A7

A5

A6

A2

A4

A1

A3

TRANSATLANTIC

Suitcase 2 Block
Template B

B3

B1

B2

B4

Photocopy at 175%

--- cut line

—— stitch line

seam allowance

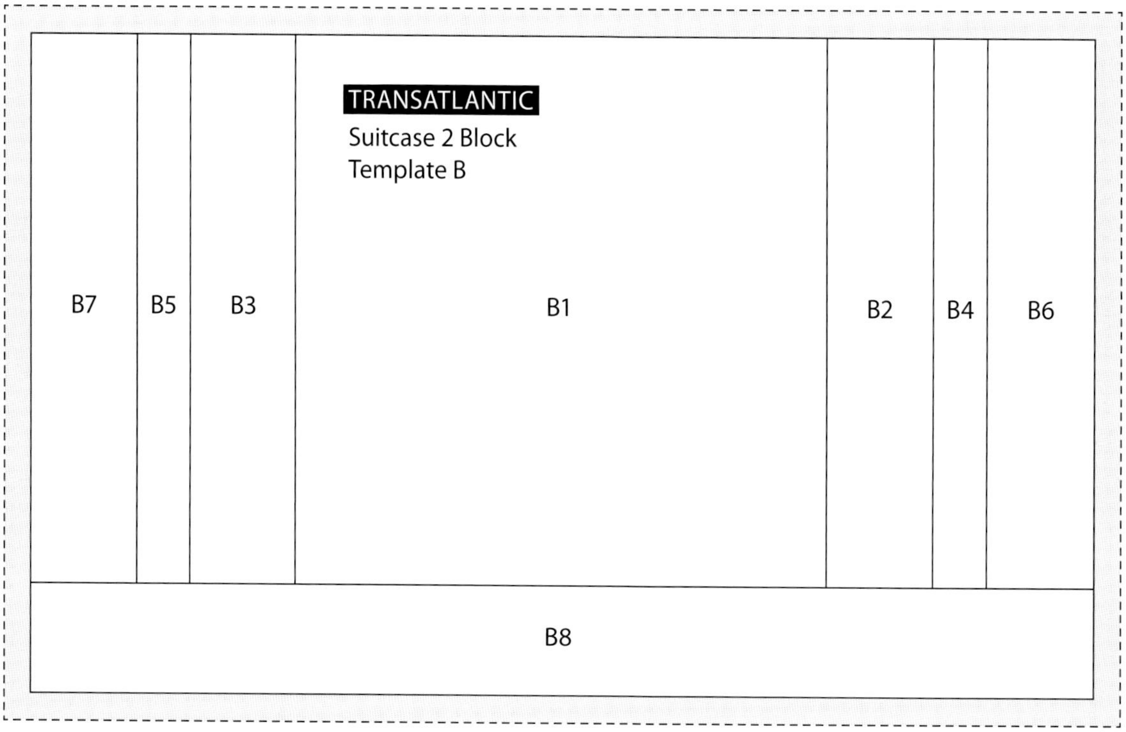

TRANSATLANTIC
Suitcase 2 Block
Template B

B7 | B5 | B3 | B1 | B2 | B4 | B6

B8

Photocopy at 175%

--- cut line

—— stitch line

seam allowance

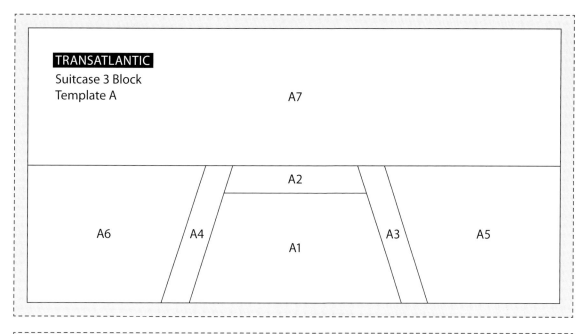

TRANSATLANTIC

Suitcase 3 Block
Template A

A7

A2

A6   A4   A1   A3   A5

TRANSATLANTIC

Suitcase 3 Block
Template B

B3   B1   B2

Photocopy at 175%

- - - cut line

—— stitch line

　　seam allowance

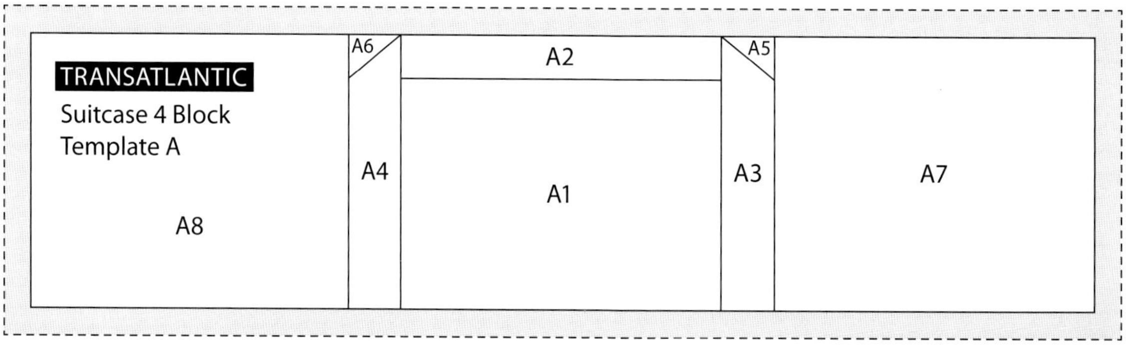

TRANSATLANTIC

Suitcase 4 Block
Template A

A6

A2

A5

A4

A1

A3

A7

A8

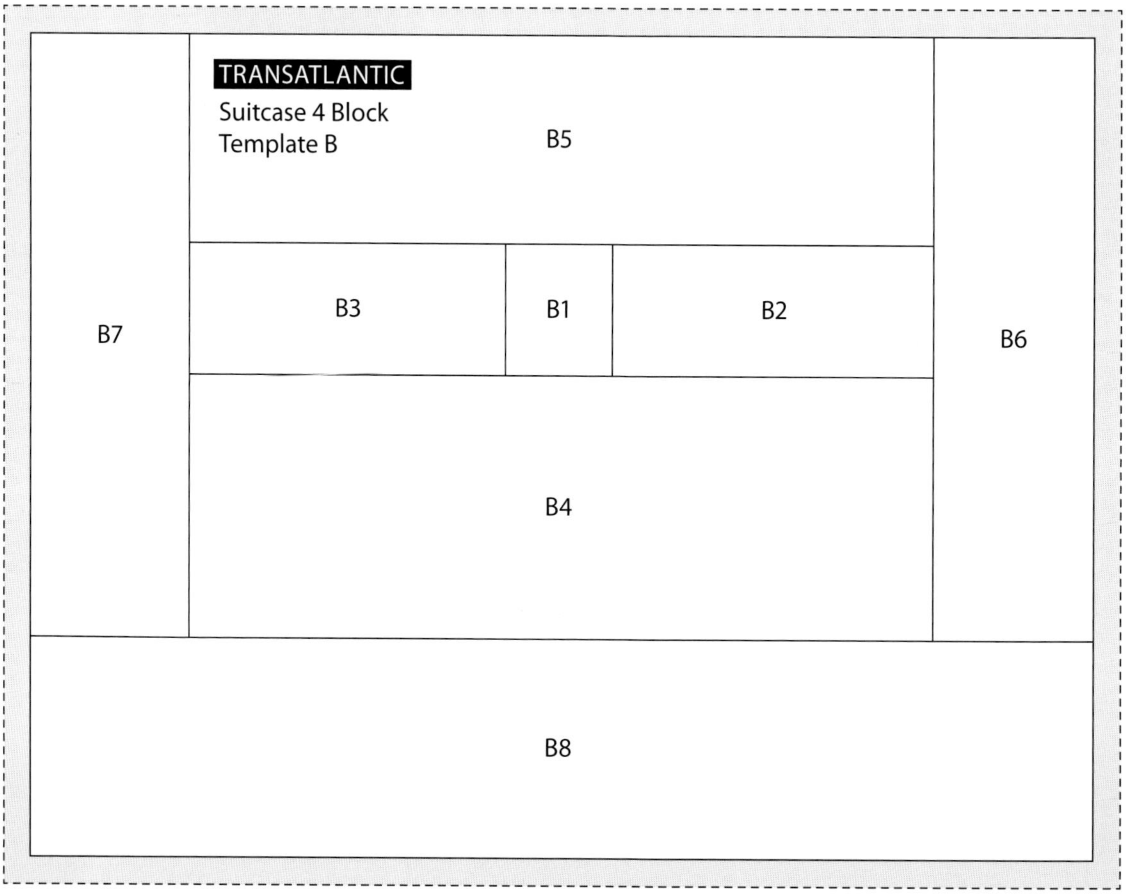

TRANSATLANTIC

Suitcase 4 Block
Template B

B5

B7

B3

B1

B2

B6

B4

B8

Photocopy at 175%

- - - cut line

—— stitch line

█ seam allowance

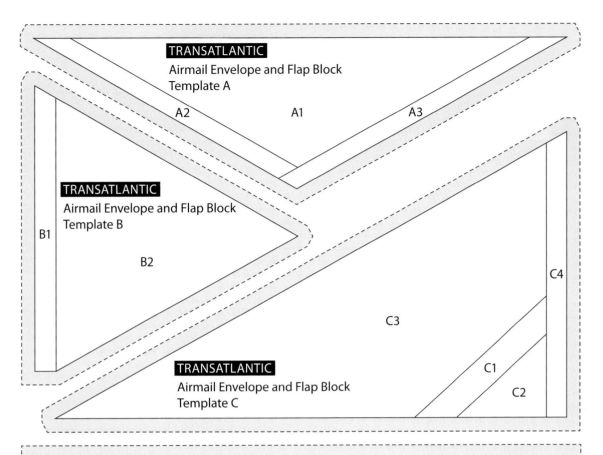

TRANSATLANTIC
Airmail Envelope and Flap Block
Template A

A2   A1   A3

TRANSATLANTIC
Airmail Envelope and Flap Block
Template B

B1

B2

C4

C3

C1

C2

TRANSATLANTIC
Airmail Envelope and Flap Block
Template C

D1

TRANSATLANTIC
Airmail Envelope and Flap Block
Template D

D2

Photocopy at 175%

--- cut line

—— stitch line

▨ seam allowance

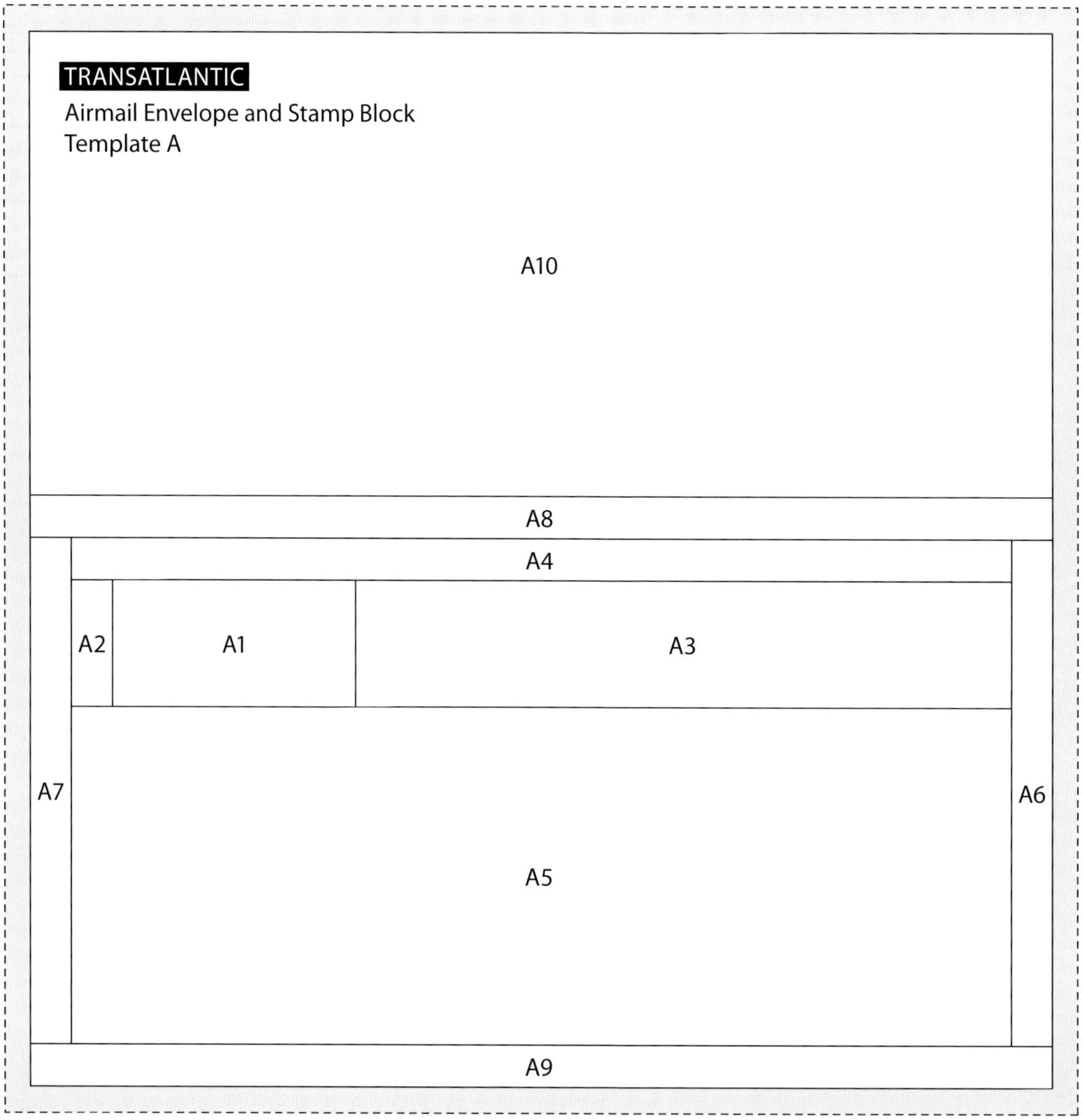

TRANSATLANTIC
Airmail Envelope and Stamp Block
Template A

A10

A8

A4

A2 A1 A3

A7 A5 A6

A9

Photocopy at 175%

- - - cut line

—— stitch line

seam allowance

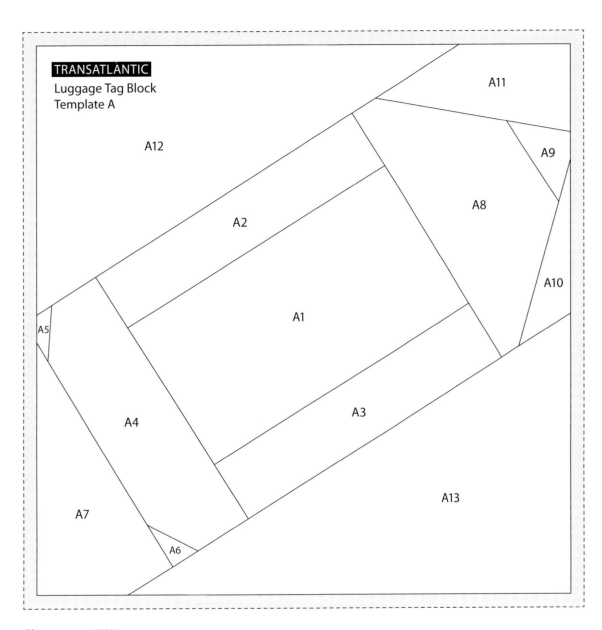

TRANSATLANTIC
Luggage Tag Block
Template A

A11

A12

A2

A9

A8

A1

A5

A10

A4

A3

A7

A13

A6

Photocopy at 175%

--- cut line

—— stitch line

seam allowance

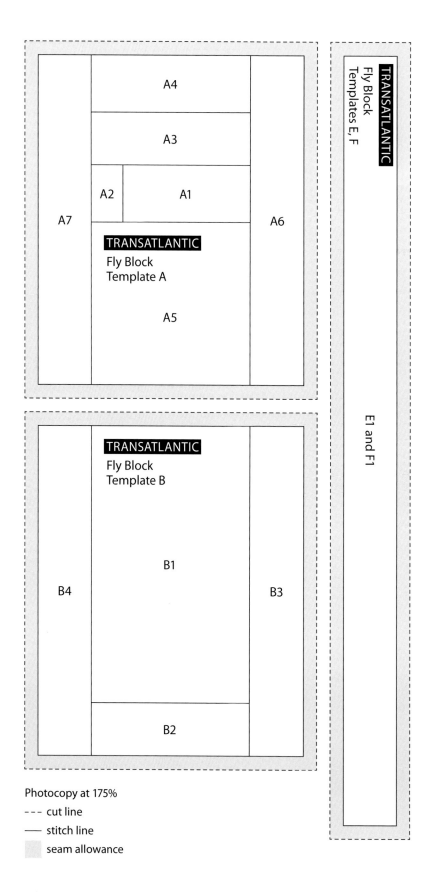

A4

A3

A2　A1

A7　A6

TRANSATLANTIC
Fly Block
Template A

A5

TRANSATLANTIC
Fly Block
Template B

B1

B4　B3

B2

TRANSATLANTIC
Fly Block
Templates E, F

E1 and F1

Photocopy at 175%

- - - cut line

——— stitch line

■ seam allowance

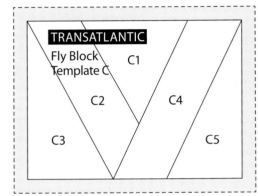

TRANSATLANTIC

Fly Block
Template C

C1

C2

C3

C4

C5

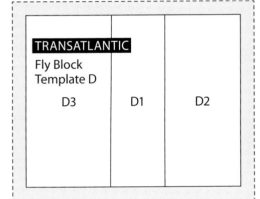

TRANSATLANTIC

Fly Block
Template D

D3

D1

D2

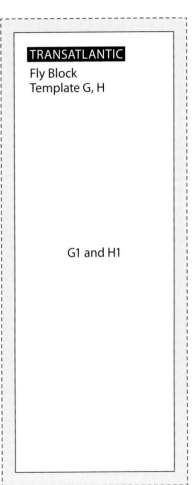

TRANSATLANTIC

Fly Block
Template G, H

G1 and H1

Photocopy at 175%

- - - cut line

—— stitch line

     seam allowance

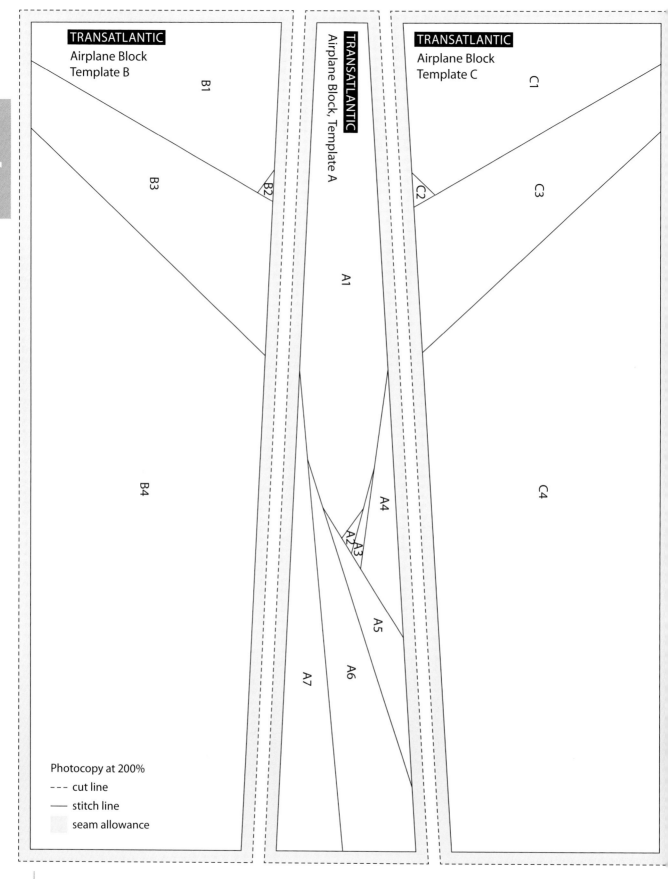

TRANSATLANTIC
Airplane Block
Template B

B1

B3

B2

B4

TRANSATLANTIC
Airplane Block, Template A

A1

A4

A2 A3

A5

A6

A7

TRANSATLANTIC
Airplane Block
Template C

C1

C2

C3

C4

Photocopy at 200%

- - - cut line

——— stitch line

■ seam allowance

Templates

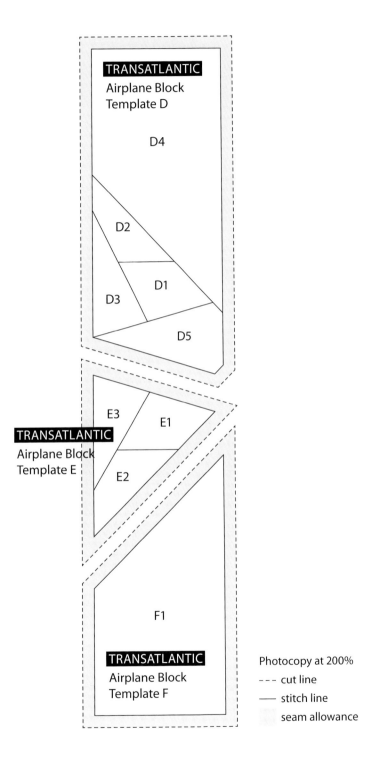

TRANSATLANTIC
Airplane Block
Template D

D4

D2

D1

D3

D5

TRANSATLANTIC
Airplane Block
Template E

E3

E1

E2

F1

TRANSATLANTIC
Airplane Block
Template F

Photocopy at 200%

- - - cut line

——— stitch line

          seam allowance

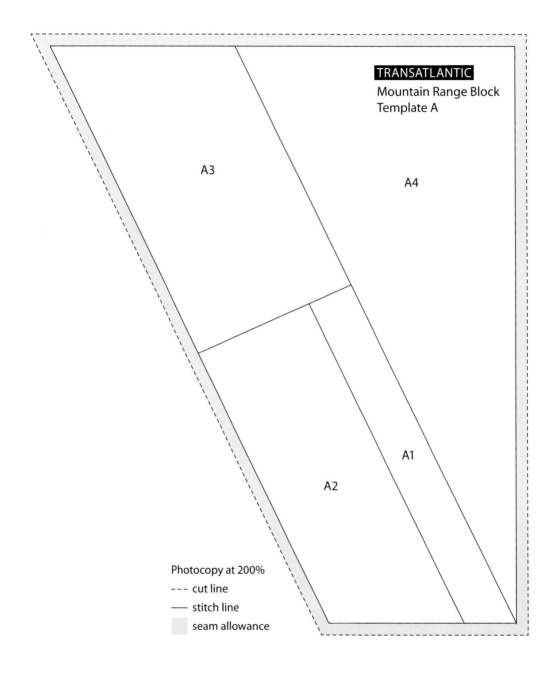

TRANSATLANTIC
Mountain Range Block
Template A

A3

A4

A1

A2

Photocopy at 200%

- - - cut line
——— stitch line
▦ seam allowance

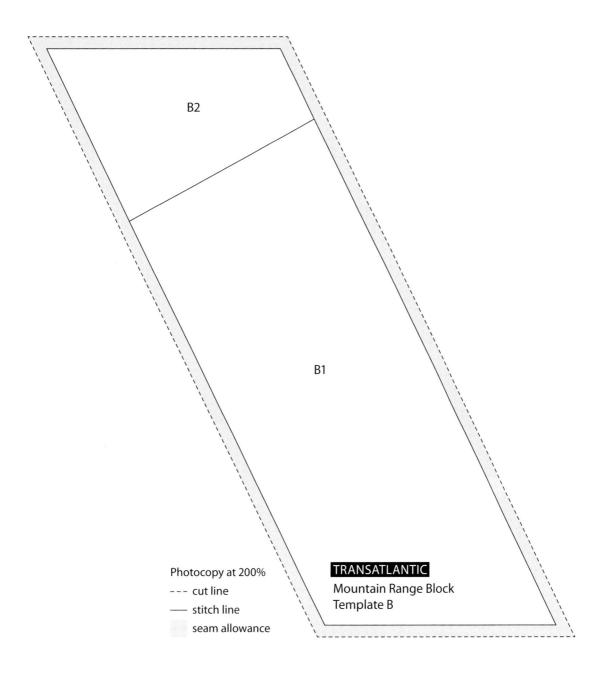

B2

B1

Photocopy at 200%

--- cut line

—— stitch line

seam allowance

TRANSATLANTIC
Mountain Range Block
Template B

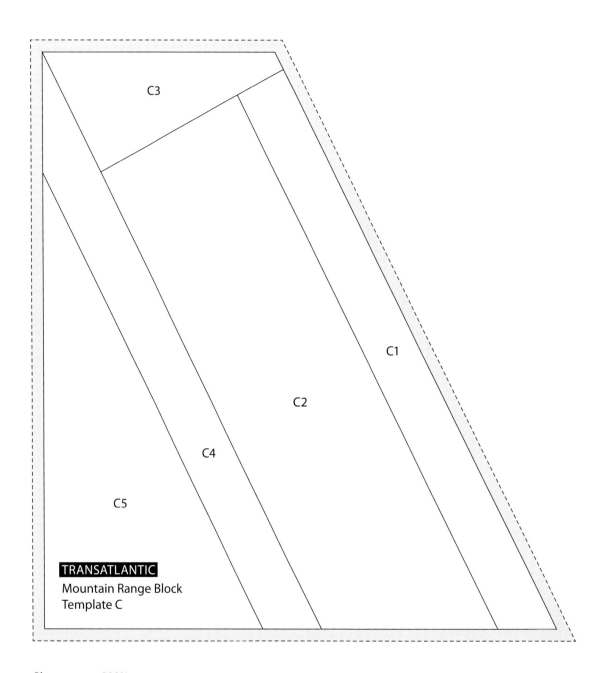

C3

C1

C2

C4

C5

TRANSATLANTIC
Mountain Range Block
Template C

Photocopy at 200%

- - - cut line

——— stitch line

seam allowance

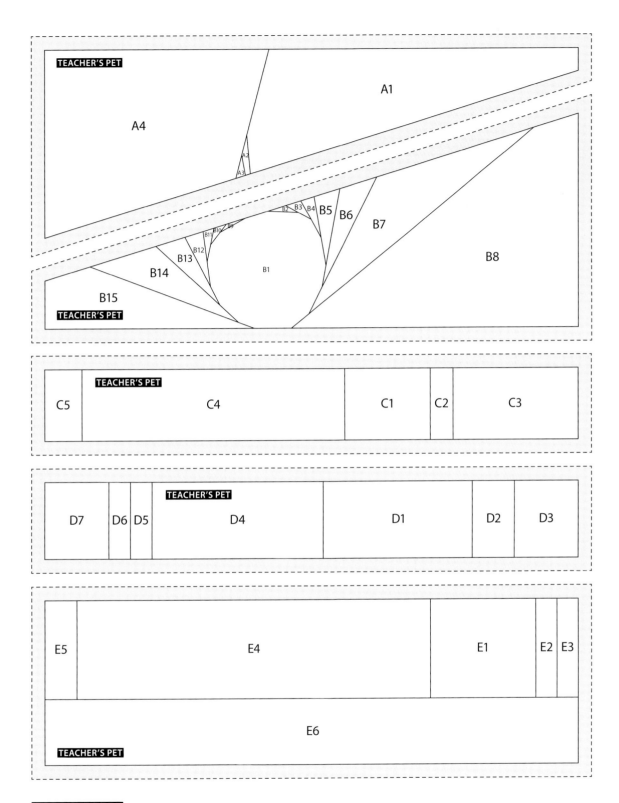

TEACHER'S PET
Block Templates

Photocopy at 175%

--- cut line
— stitch line
   seam allowance

Templates

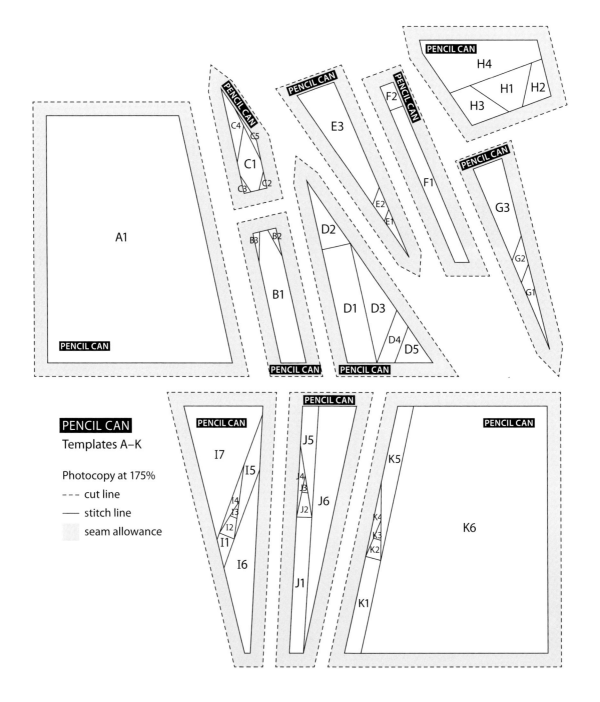

PENCIL CAN

Templates A–K

Photocopy at 175%

--- cut line
— stitch line
░ seam allowance

Templates

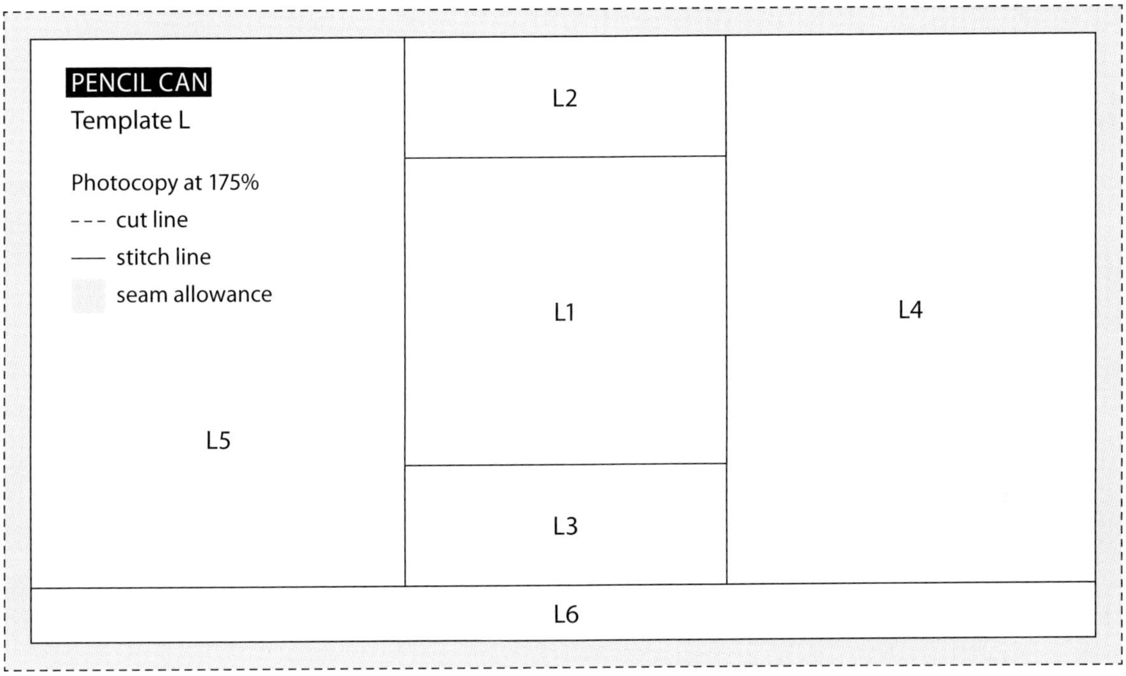

PENCIL CAN

Template L

Photocopy at 175%

- - - cut line

——— stitch line

⬚ seam allowance

L2

L1

L3

L4

L5

L6

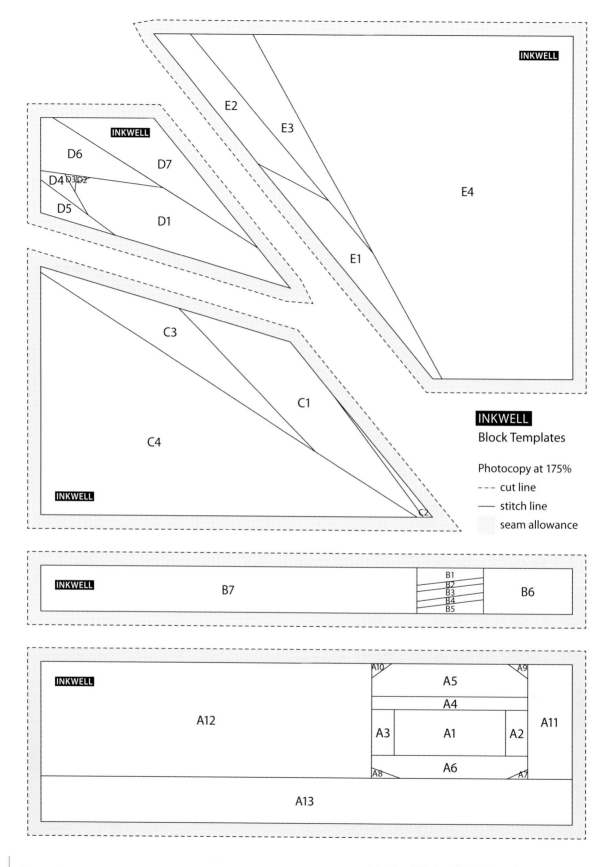

INKWELL

INKWELL

INKWELL

INKWELL
Block Templates

Photocopy at 175%
- - - cut line
—— stitch line
seam allowance

INKWELL

INKWELL

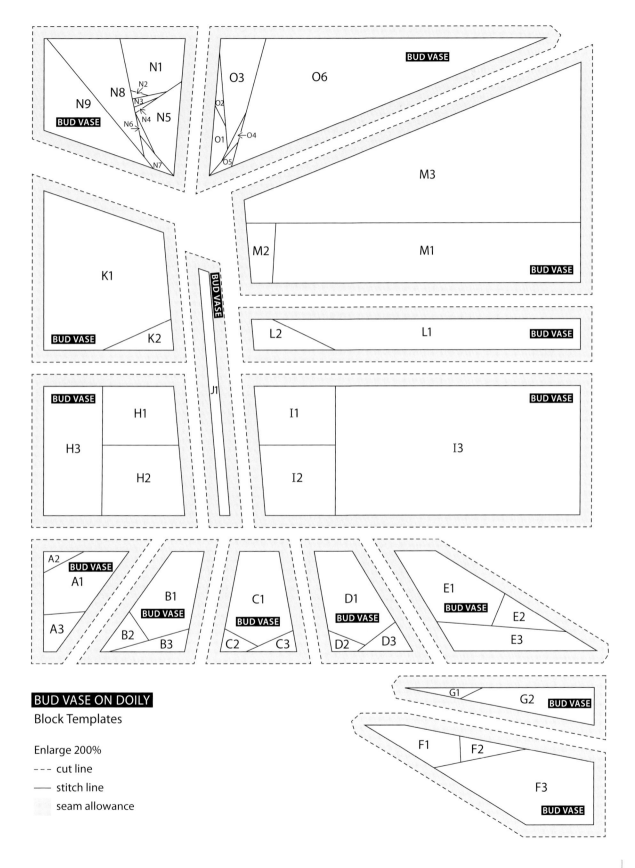

BUD VASE ON DOILY

Block Templates

Enlarge 200%

- - - cut line

——— stitch line

seam allowance

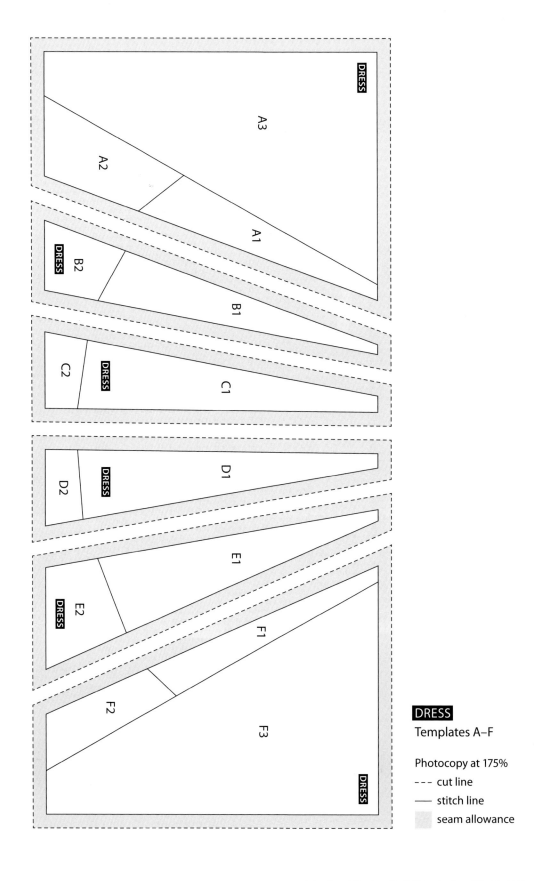

DRESS
Templates A–F

Photocopy at 175%
--- cut line
— stitch line
seam allowance

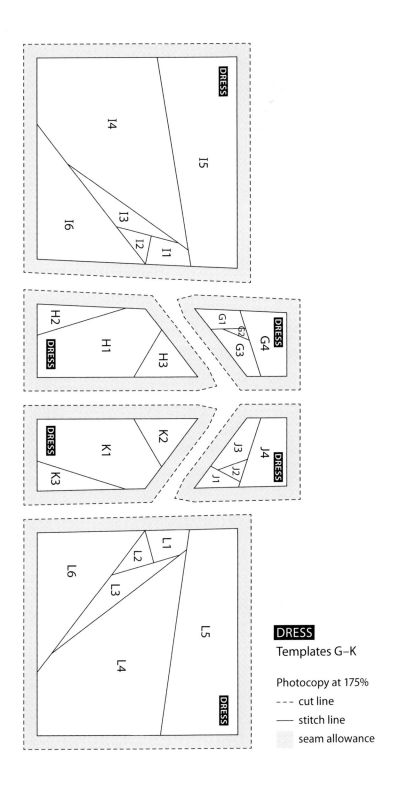

DRESS

Templates G–K

Photocopy at 175%

- - - cut line
—— stitch line
▨ seam allowance

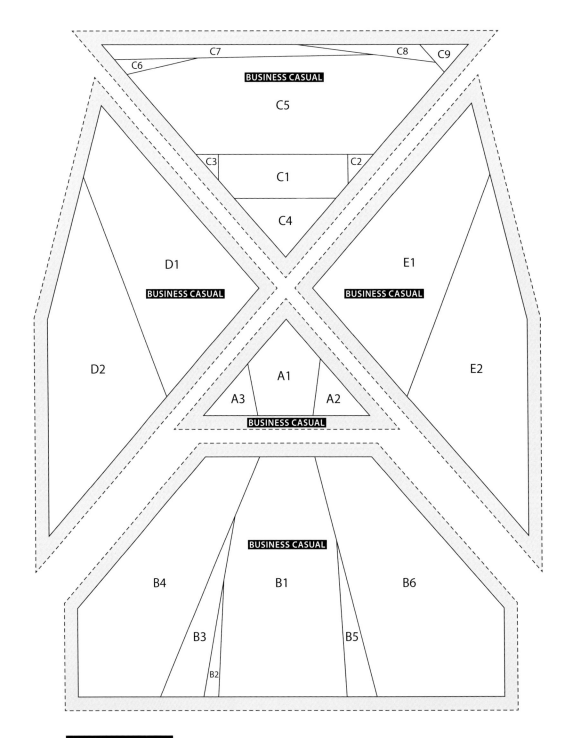

BUSINESS CASUAL

Templates A–E

Photocopy at 175%

- - - cut line

—— stitch line

    seam allowance

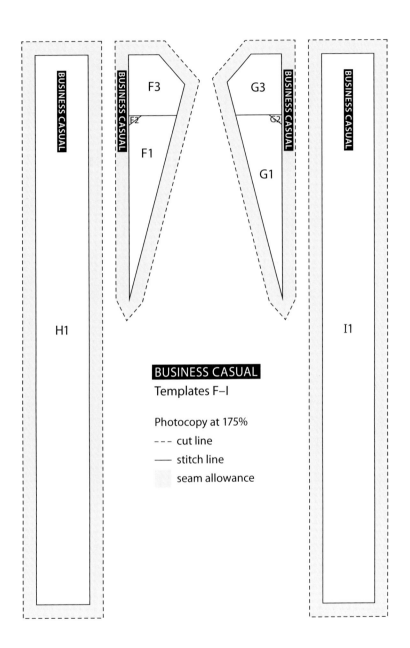

H1

BUSINESS CASUAL

F3

F2

F1

G3

G2

G1

I1

BUSINESS CASUAL

BUSINESS CASUAL

Templates F–I

Photocopy at 175%

- - - cut line
——— stitch line
⬜ seam allowance

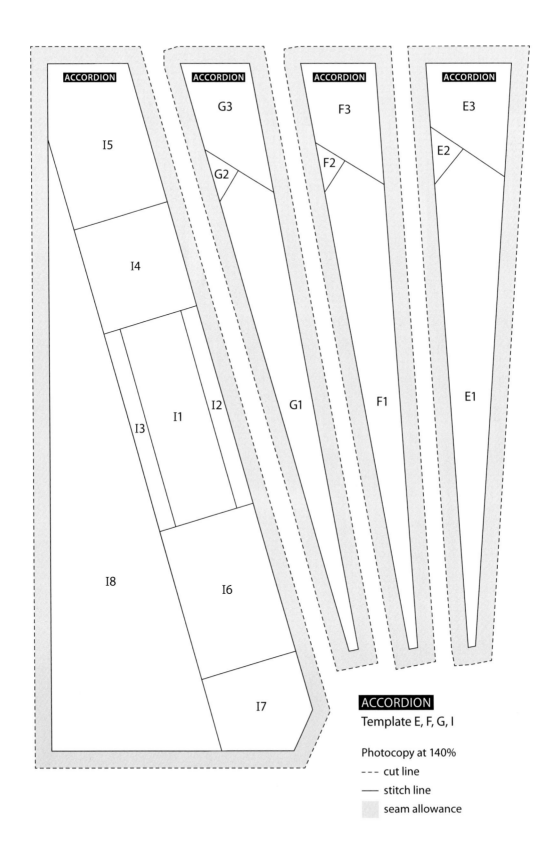

ACCORDION

Template E, F, G, I

Photocopy at 140%

- - - cut line

—— stitch line

seam allowance

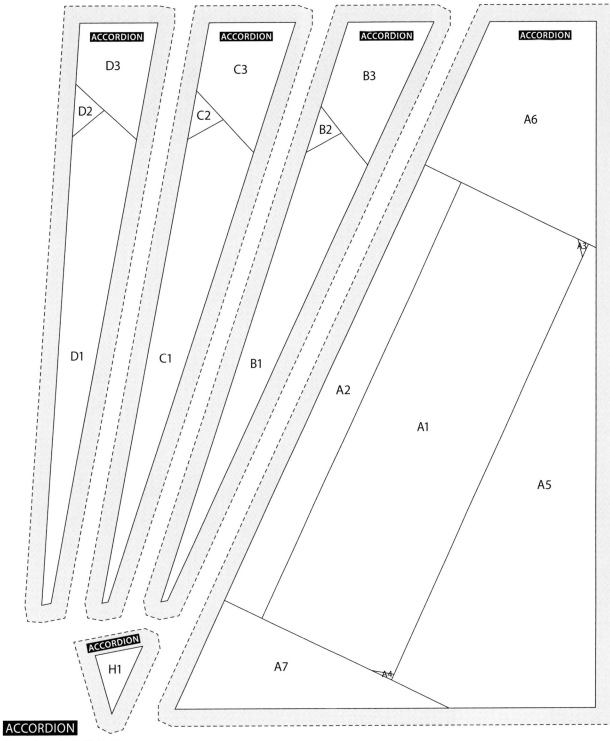

ACCORDION
D3

ACCORDION
C3

ACCORDION
B3

ACCORDION
A6

D2

C2

B2

D1

C1

B1

A2

A1

A3

A5

ACCORDION
H1

A7

A4

ACCORDION
Template A, B, C, D, H

Photocopy at 140%

- - - cut line

——— stitch line

seam allowance

Templates

Templates

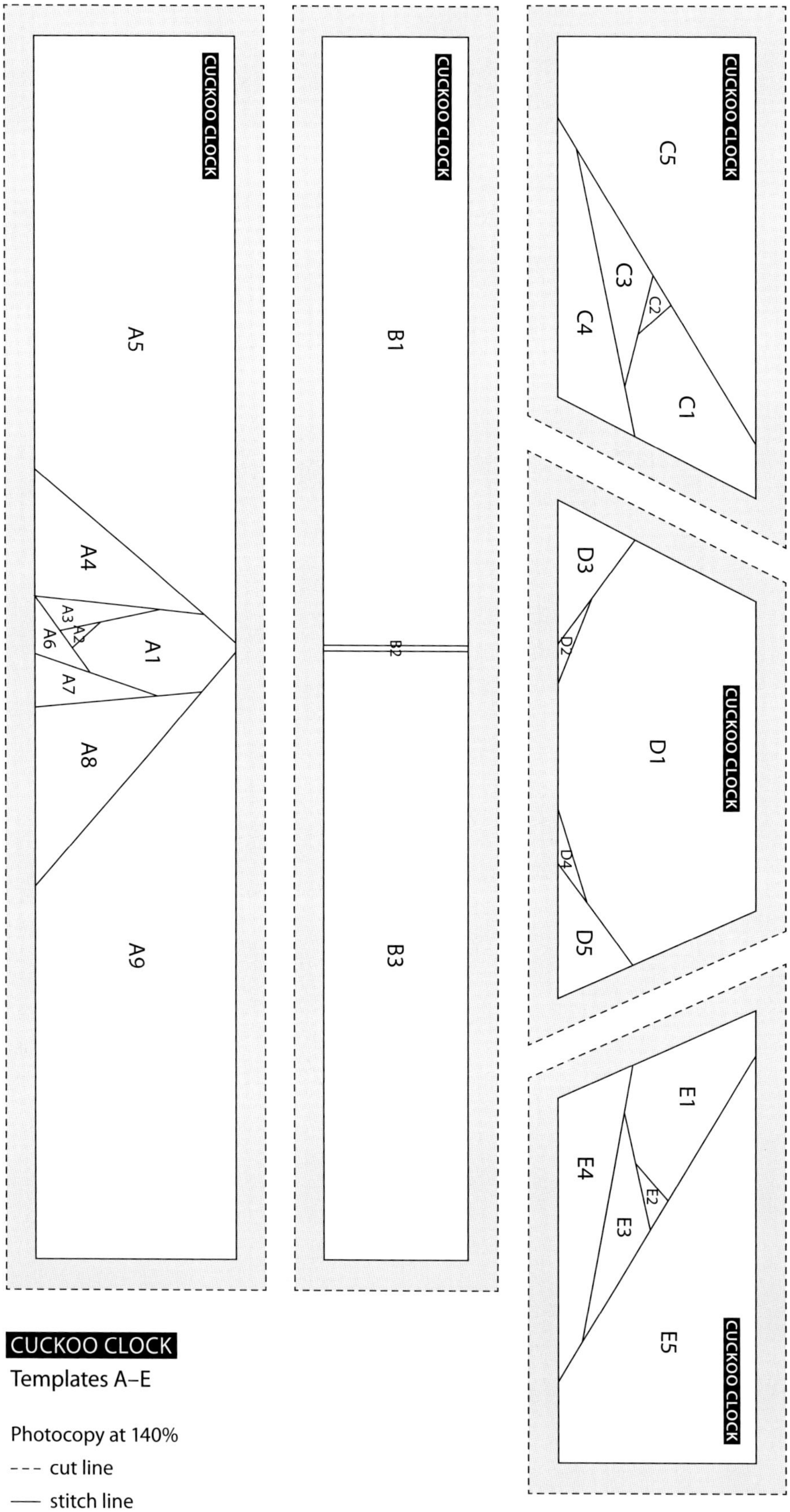
CUCKOO CLOCK
A5
A4
A3
A2
A6
A1
A7
A8
A9
CUCKOO CLOCK
B1
B2
B3
CUCKOO CLOCK
C5
C3
C2
C4
C1
D3
D2
CUCKOO CLOCK
D1
D4
D5
E1
E4
E2
E3
E5
CUCKOO CLOCK

CUCKOO CLOCK

Templates A–E

Photocopy at 140%

--- cut line

—— stitch line

seam allowance

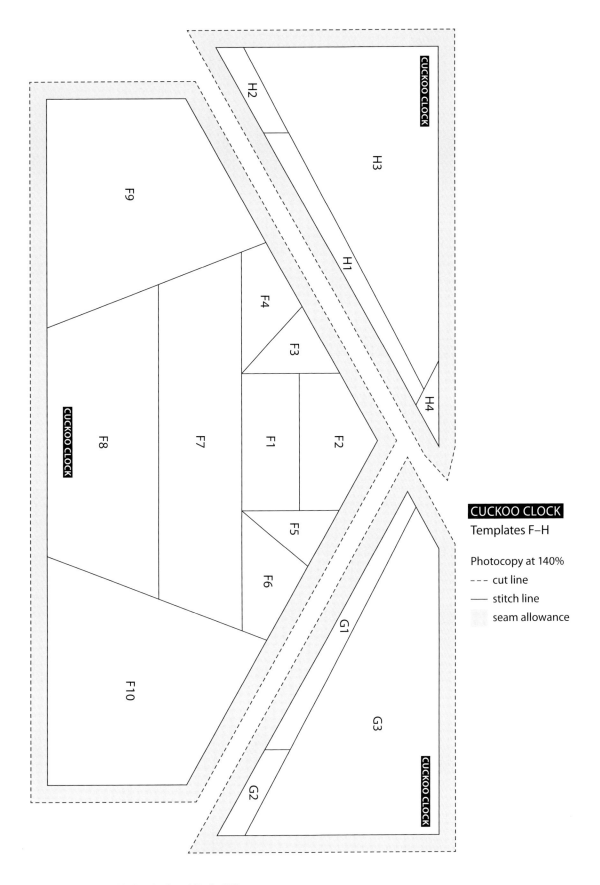

CUCKOO CLOCK

Templates F–H

Photocopy at 140%
- - - cut line
—— stitch line
░ seam allowance

H2
H3
CUCKOO CLOCK
H1
H4
F4
F3
F9
F7
F8
CUCKOO CLOCK
F1
F2
F5
F6
G1
F10
G3
CUCKOO CLOCK
G2

LAUNDRY TUB

Block Templates

Photocopy at 200%

- - - cut line
—— stitch line
▓ seam allowance

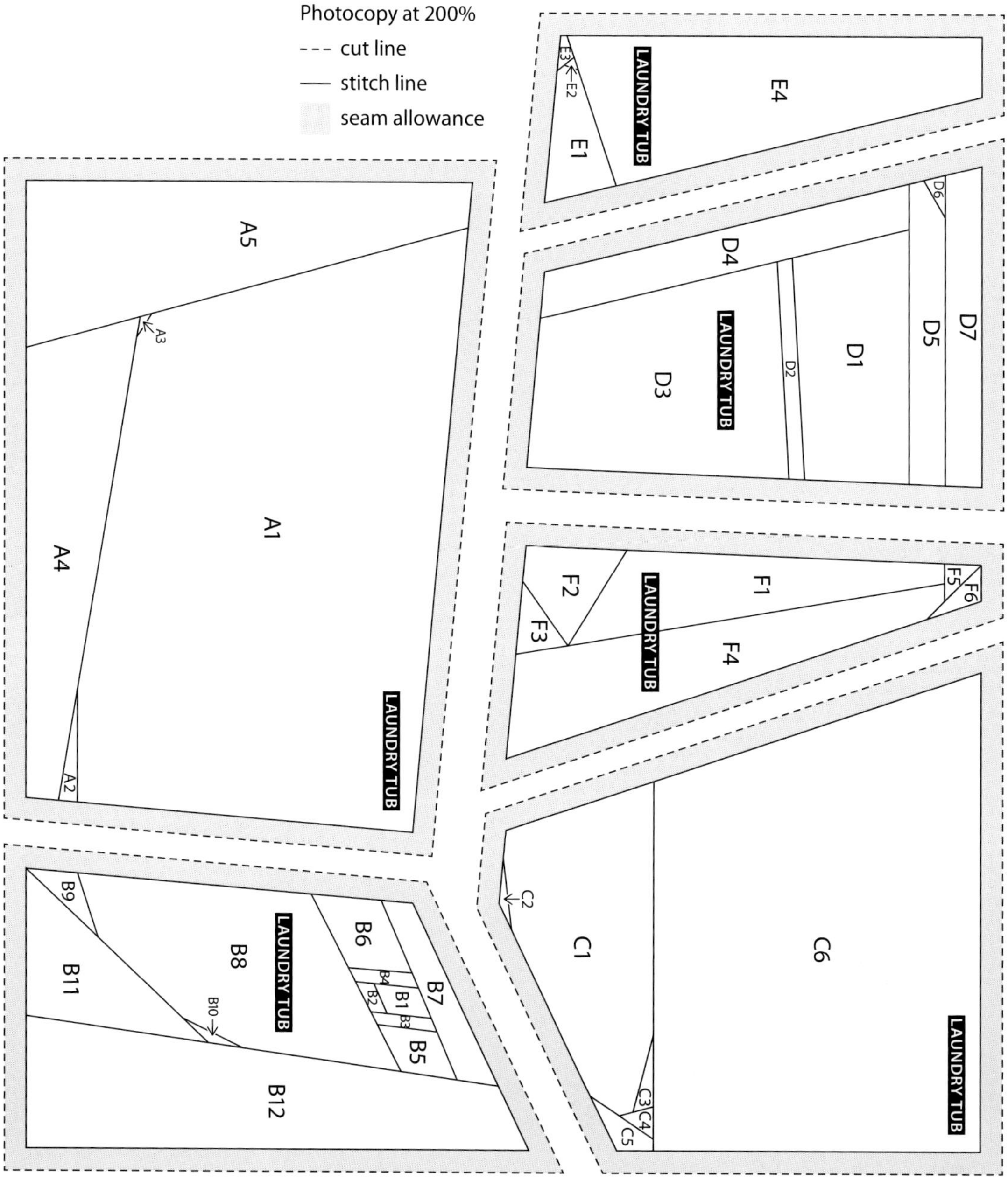

LAUNDRY TUB

E4

E1

E3 ←E2

LAUNDRY TUB

D6

D4

D7

D5

D1

D2

LAUNDRY TUB

D3

A5

A3

A1

A4

A2

LAUNDRY TUB

F2

F3

F1

LAUNDRY TUB

F4

F5

F6

C2

C1

C6

C3 C4

C5

LAUNDRY TUB

B9

B6

B8

LAUNDRY TUB

B7

B4 B1 B3

B2

B5

B10

B11

B12

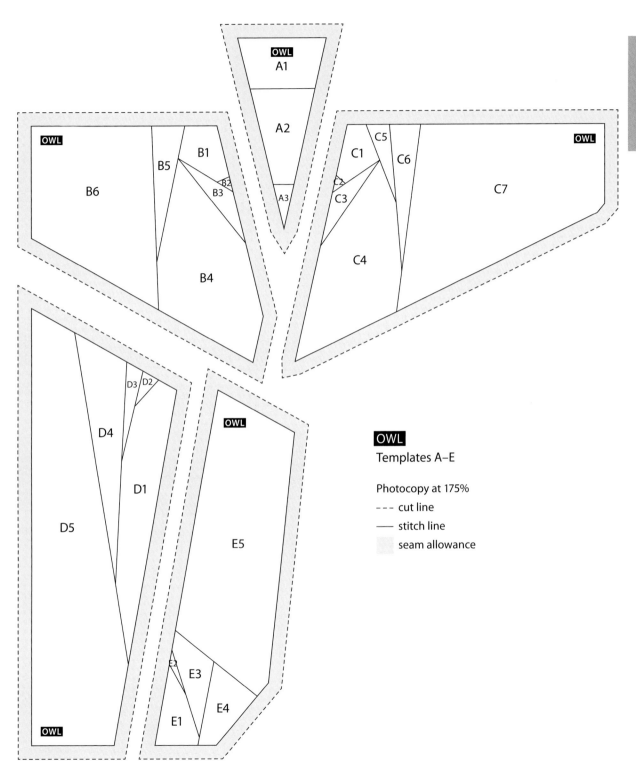

OWL

Templates A–E

Photocopy at 175%

--- cut line

— stitch line

▨ seam allowance

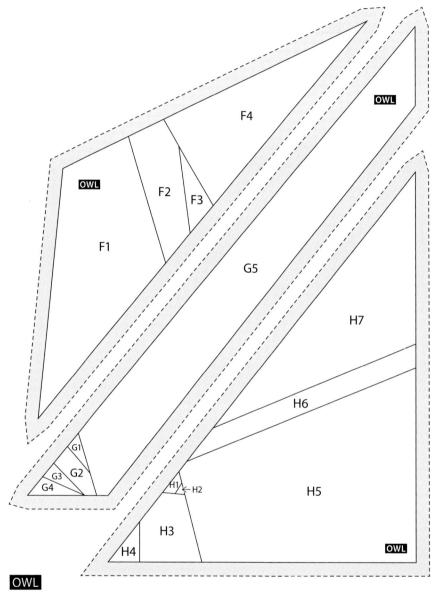

F4

OWL

OWL

F2

F3

F1

G5

H7

H6

H5

G1

G3 G2

G4

H1 H2

H3

H4

OWL

OWL

Templates F–H

Photocopy at 175%

- - - cut line

—— stitch line

▨ seam allowance

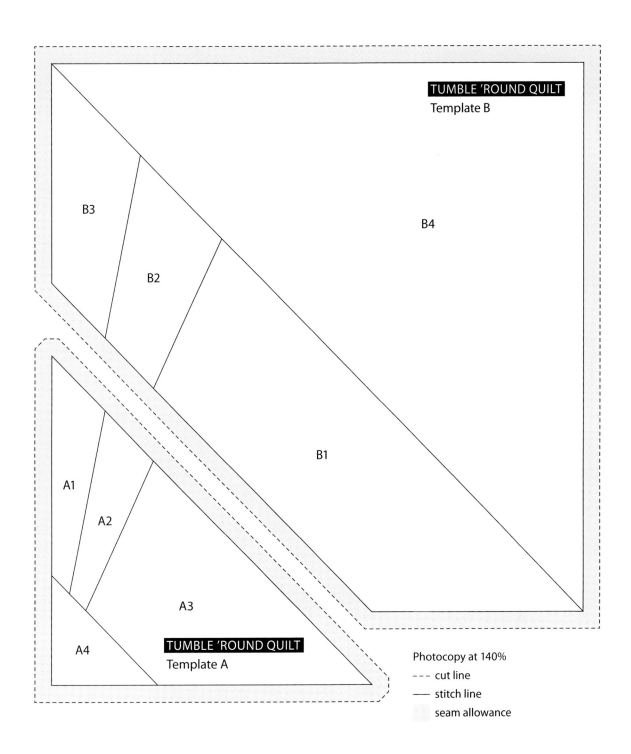

TUMBLE 'ROUND QUILT
Template B

B3

B4

B2

B1

A1

A2

A3

A4

TUMBLE 'ROUND QUILT
Template A

Photocopy at 140%

--- cut line

— stitch line

seam allowance

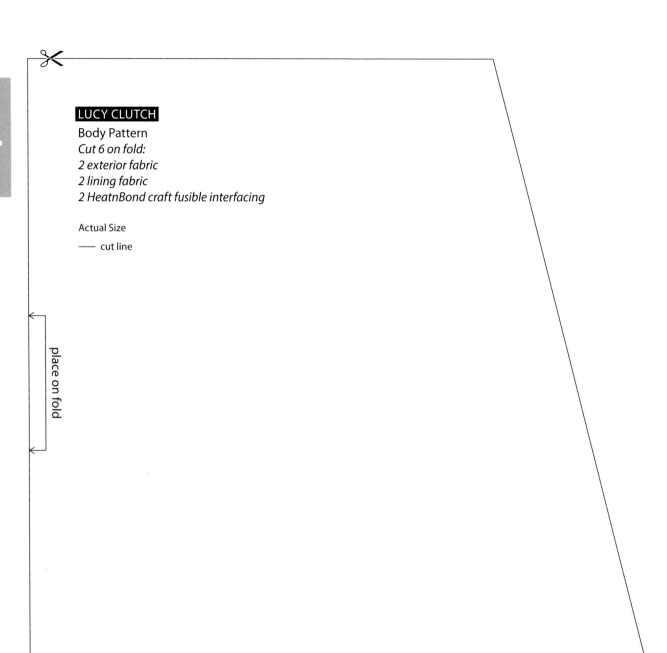

LUCY CLUTCH

Body Pattern

Cut 6 on fold:
2 exterior fabric
2 lining fabric
2 HeatnBond craft fusible interfacing

Actual Size

—— cut line

place on fold

Templates

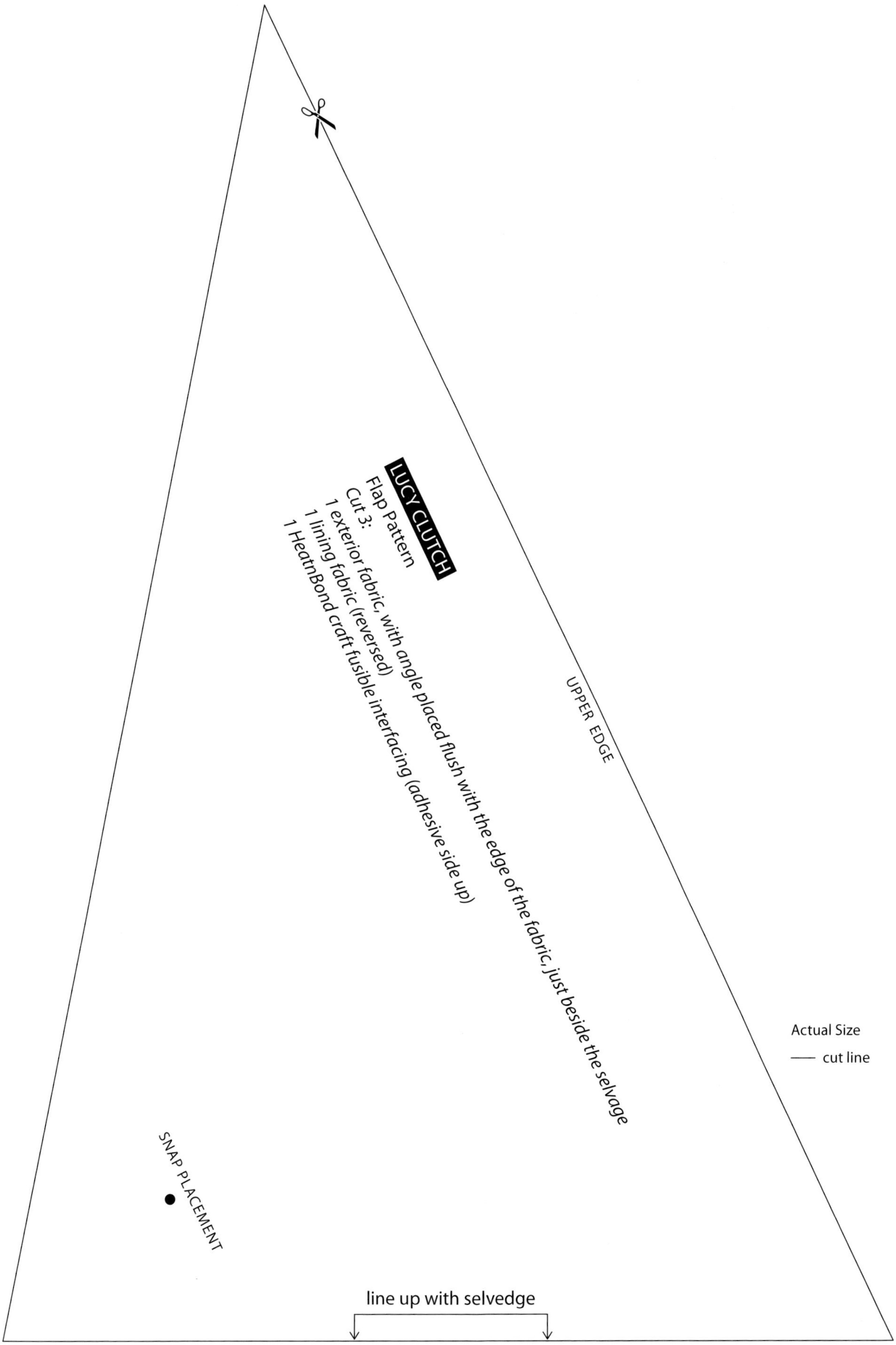

LUCY CLUTCH

Flap Pattern
Cut 3:
1 exterior fabric, with angle placed flush with the edge of the fabric, just beside the selvage
1 lining fabric (reversed)
1 HeatnBond craft fusible interfacing (adhesive side up)

UPPER EDGE

Actual Size
—— cut line

SNAP PLACEMENT
●

line up with selvedge

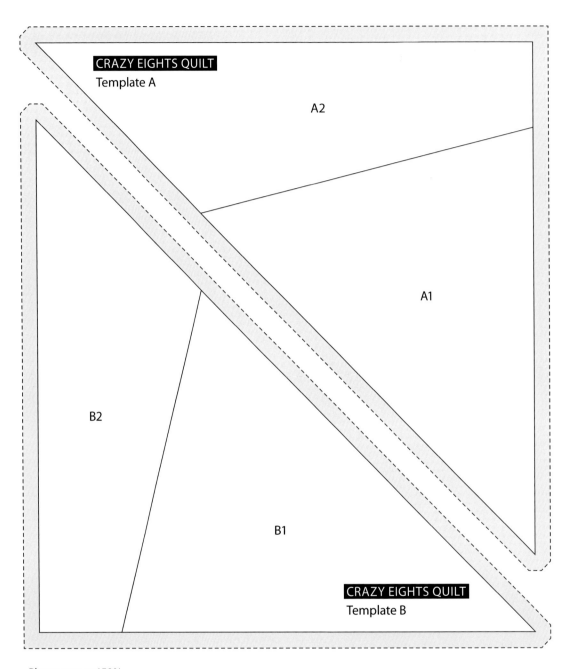

CRAZY EIGHTS QUILT
Template A

A2

A1

B2

B1

CRAZY EIGHTS QUILT
Template B

Photocopy at 150%

--- cut line

——— stitch line

seam allowance

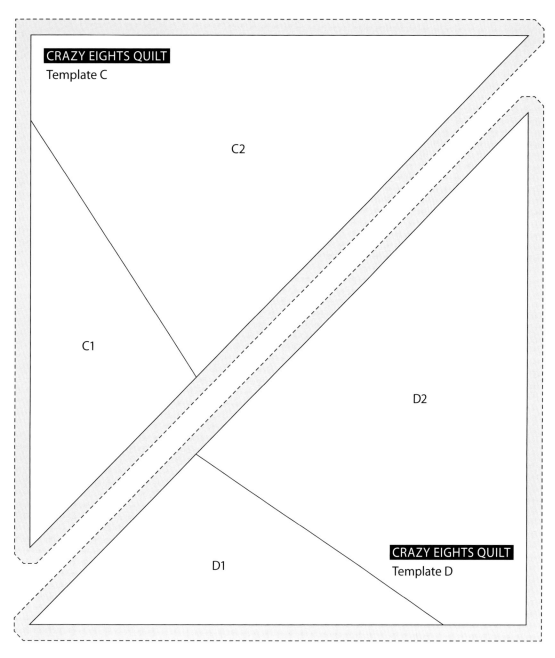

CRAZY EIGHTS QUILT
Template C

C2

C1

D2

CRAZY EIGHTS QUILT
Template D

D1

Photocopy at 150%

--- cut line

—— stitch line

  seam allowance